# THE RISE OF THE UNICORN

eHappyPedia

by LINKEDIN AND TOWN HALL ACHIEVER OF THE YEAR
EY NOMINEE ENTREPRENEUR OF THE YEAR
GRAND HOMAGE LYS DIVERSITY

## Dr. BAK NGUYEN, DMD

&

by MANAGER OF THE YEAR, ESG-UQAM

## Dr. JEAN DE SERRES, MD, MBA

TO ALL WHO ARE DREAMING OF HAPPINESS AND A BETTER WORLD.
TO ALL OF THOSE DREAMING OF A NEW WAY TO COMMUNICATE.

by Dr. BAK NGUYEN
& Dr. JEAN DE SERRES

# ABOUT THE AUTHORS

From Canada, **Dr. BAK NGUYEN**, Nominee Ernst and Young Entrepreneur of the year, Grand Homage Lys DIVERSITY, LinkedIn & TownHall Achiever of the year and TOP 100 Doctors 2021. Dr Bak is a cosmetic dentist, CEO and founder of Mdex & Co. His company is revolutionizing the dental field. Speaker and motivator, he wrote 72 books over 36 months accumulating many world records (to be officialized).

- **ENTREPRENEURSHIP**
- **LEADERSHIP**
- **QUEST OF IDENTITY**
- **DENTISTRY AND MEDICINE**
- **PARENTING**
- **CHILDREN BOOKS**
- **PHILOSOPHY**

In 2003, he founded Mdex, a dental company upon which in 2018, he launched the most ambitious private endeavour to reform the dental industry, Canada wide. Philosopher, he has close to his heart the quest of happiness of the people surrounding him, patients and colleagues alike. In 2020, he launched an International collaborative initiative named **THE ALPHAS** to share knowledge and for Entrepreneurs and Doctors to thrive through the Greatest Pandemic and Economic depression of our time.

In 2016, he co-found with Tranie Vo, Emotive World Incorporated, a tech research company to use technology to empower happiness and sharing. U.A.X. the ultimate audio experience is the landmark project on which the team is advancing, utilizing the technics of the movie industry and the advancement in ARTIFICIAL INTELLIGENCE to save the book industry and to upgrade the continuing education space.

These projects have allowed Dr Nguyen to attract interests from the international and diplomatic community and he is now the center of a global discussion in the wellbeing and the future of the health profession. It is in that matter that he shares his thoughts and encourages the health community to share their own stories.

"It's not worth it go through it alone! Together, we stand, alone, we fall."

Motivational speaker and serial entrepreneur, philosopher and author, from his own words, Dr Nguyen describes himself as a dentist by circumstances, an entrepreneur by nature and a communicator by passion.

He also holds recognitions from the Canadian Parliament and the Canadian Senate.

From Canada, **Dr. JEAN DE SERRES**, ESG/UQAM, MANAGER OF THE YEAR. Dr. De Serres is a MD with MBA and Master degree in public health. He has been a family physician, a CEO, a board administrator, an entrepreneur, a speaker and a teacher. Dr. De Serres is the former CEO of Hema Quebec.

He also created a clinic for victims of sexual abuse. Currently VP in a pharmaceutical company, his main focus is the change of organizational culture and innovation.

# THE RISE OF THE UNICORN

eHappyPedia

by Dr. BAK NGUYEN
& Dr. JEAN DE SERRES

CONCLUSION
BY Dr. JEAN DE SERRES

10

# ACKNOWLEDGEMENTS

by Dr. BAK NGUYEN

For all of you who are following my writings, you already know I'm exposing my past, my thoughts, and my daily. All that is mentioned in my books are things that I am doing. But this book is different.

**THE RISE OF THE UNICORN** is the initiative of Dr. Jean De Serres, my friend, and mentor who wanted a way for us to communicate, share and bring back to life a great project that I started earlier and that I left on the back burner: **eHappyPedia**.

Within the next chapters, you will explore the story of a great company that we tried to build, but also what we should have done and might be doing, once more, to bring it back to life. This book is part real, part projection.

The real value of it was that it revived the interest and attention of Jean and myself for one of our dreams. To you, it is of value since you will experience not only a great storyline but also the technics that a mentor is deploying to motivate and resuscitate an old flame.

On that, **UNICORN** was a title proposed by Jean, because this is what it really is: a **UNICORN**, a multi-million dollar idea, one that can change the world for the better! The expression describes both a dream and a reality, a business success!

I really hope that you will enjoy your journey following our discussion and our projections. By the time of this writing, parts of this book are still projections. But you know me, give me some time, and we will make the story a reality!

Enjoy.

Dr. Bak Nguyen

# PROLOGUE

## "A DREAM OR A REALITY?"

by Dr. JEAN DE SERRES

A dreamer is building the future. What is reality and what is dream? Is what on your mind real or a fake? Is that future real? A unicorn is a fictional character for kids but to some parents, it is really real! It is happiness and life. It also serves a function in the development of that kid and his future.

A Unicorn is a union of two animals : a horse and a rhinoceros. It has been part of our culture since Antiquity and transferred throughout time and space. We can find Unicorns related stories in the middle age and even in modern North Korea.

A Unicorn is also an issue when it is a target impossible to reach like they say about recruitment of a world star staff for an ordinary job. It seems neither real or fake, but more like a mistake... (or a sign of incompetence?). Or a dream with no possibility of realization.

But a Unicorn can be something else, something much higher. In the finance world, a Unicorn is also the hope of many VCs : a private company worth a Billion $.

There have been many of these in recent years : Google, Facebook, Uber, Airbnb and some more. Although overall, analysts say it is rare as this happens to 0.07 % of companies, in other words, only one company in 1400 will rise as a Unicorn.

A Unicorn is certainly a target for investors and for business people launching new companies. Not as rare as in the Human Resources department, in finance, a Unicorn is definitely a target, a possibility. Many not possible nor accessible to everyone, but surely a possibility.

So a Unicorn is mostly MANY things in one : a company that succeeds like crazy, a dream, a child fantasy, a mistake.

"FROM THE MANY COMES THE POSSIBLE!"
Dr. JEAN DE SERRES

Maybe that is why a Unicorn can be a target and a dream. All those different definitions are talking about the boundaries of now and of the future, of thoughts (whether dreams, or childlike intelligence or bad decisions) and, of course, of reality!

There are 2 dimensions about the Unicorns : time and human thinking. Time where the reality of today is the result of the past, where the future is being constructed today. Human thinking with discussions, planning, creativity.

"WHERE AND WHAT IS THE REALITY IS NOT SO IMPORTANT
BECAUSE THE FUTURE STARTS WITH DREAMS!"
Dr. JEAN DE SERRES

Because the future is built from ideas, imagination and with drive. Humanity needs hope and hope can only exist when the future can be dreamed!

A UNICORN is thus MANY things.
A UNICORN is MANY POSSIBLE.
A UNICORN is DREAM
A UNICORN is CREATION
A UNICORN is HUMAN!

This book is about the reality of Unicorns in the shape of a company. The story and the essay are also unicorns. This is a normal... in the world of Unicorns, in the world of possibilities!


Dr. Jean De Serres

# INTRODUCTION
"GOOD THINGS START TO HAPPEN WHEN YOU SAY YES!"

by Dr. BAK NGUYEN

This is the first time in days since I last picked up my iPhone to write. Even the letters on the keyboard seem different, like they are getting smaller. I can tell you that it feels good to be back.

9 days to be exact since I finished the last chapter and the conclusion of **SELFMADE**, my 35th opus, which is now online on the iTunes store! I know, I make it sound dramatic, but to me, hours feel like days, and days feel like weeks.

Less than three weeks ago, I was on vacation in the Dominican Republic wrapping up my 35th and 36th book, **SELFMADE** and **THE POWER OF YES volume 1**. And now with **SELFMADE**, I signed up for my first solo speaking event, the first Dr. Bak's event.

In other words, people will be showing up to hear me speaking, not to discover me... My team has booked one of the biggest and classiest auditorium in Montreal, the Center Mont-Royal, former United Nations' convention center.

We are expecting close to 700 people! For a first event solo, that's a lot of people... Needless to say that I am nervous! And I hope logistic will work! But that's not my job. My job is to inspire, not to sell. That's why I have a team under the leadership of business strategist, Jonas Diop.

It may be a Dr. Bak's event, but loyal to my character, I will not simply seize the day without sharing what I hold dear. I will be sharing my journey saying **YES** by default, discovering my talents as an author and scoring world record over world record, and will be introducing 3 of my *protégés* to the public.

These are people that have joined me and embraced Life with an open mind: Business coach and strategist Jonas Diop, fitness coach Dino Masson and a young prodigy, William Bak, my son.

I am proud to introduce all of them to you since they are living proofs that with WILLPOWER and an open mind, Life can change within weeks and days.

So far, a third of the tickets were gone within 10 days. Not bad for three weeks since vacation, but that's not all!

At **Mdex & Co**, things are picking up. We had never been so popular among patients and dentists. We worked hard for it, and now the blessings are at our doors.

A year ago, we opened a new concept and a new economic model. Today, I am pleased to report that we lack space… even with two floors in a prime real estate high rise on the Golden Square Mile, in the heart of Montreal.

With the signatures of partners and the incoming of patients, it's just not possible to be exempt from the frenzy and the excitement! Not to forget that we just confirmed the financing for a new complex in downtown Montreal. Yes, a second one!

I am at the office 5 days a week from 9:30 AM to sometimes 11 PM, meeting with partners and drafting the future. You wanted to know how an entrepreneur spends his days? Just go through my introductions, from book to book, to have my diary as an entrepreneur and author.

And with my wife's help, I finally got through my publishing issues with Apple and iTune. My books are now internationally distributed, reaching 51 countries on the Apple Books' store in less than 12 hours after I've pressed send.

This is a huge step forward! It means I am closer than ever to my readers: there won't be anyone anymore between you and me. I write, I correct, I edit, and I send. Sure my team will be doing their work too, but those will be updates and improvements.

Knowing that I do not see my misspelling, my team now runs at my pace, sometimes a little behind, to polish and correct my releases, now that they are hitting the markets at Dr. Bak's pace! It helps me to keep my *speed* and **momentum**.

So I spent the last weeks editing and proofreading three of my opus: **PROFESSION HEALTH**, my 5th, **SELFMADE**, my 35th and **CHANGING THE WORLD FROM A DENTAL CHAIR**, my 7th. Those three are now available on iTunes. I am pushing myself to edit two books a week, but that's not a promise, it is an unrealistic goal and an optimistic hope.

With 3 world records writing 37 books, editing and proofreading are mind-numbing to me. It requires way more attention and energy than writing if you ask me. But, I'll do it. Do whatever it takes, right?

But something is missing. For the last week, I haven't written a single word, and I am growing frustrated with the void. Writing is not a side anymore, it has become an *aptitude* and a *habit*. I just need something to write about, as soon as I can put aside the editing.

That's when Dr. Jean De Serres, my dear friend and mentor came to the rescue. Since the beginning of my journey as an author, I wanted to sign a book with him.

He signed the preface of my first book, **SYMPHONY OF SKILLS**, encouraged me to keep going, even accepted to be interviewed for a chapter in **PROFESSION HEALTH**, but it is just lately that he agreed to co-sign a book with me.

**eHappyPedia, THE RISE OF THE UNICORN**, that's our book together, my 37th opus.

A few years ago, I started **eHappyPedia**, an online platform where people can share recipes of happiness and stories of joy. It had a great start but needed more resources and attention... We needed more or less 10 million in funds. Resources and attention I diverted to **Mdex & Co**.

Jean was part of that adventure. Today, he wants us to put back that project of happiness at the center of our attention. **eHappyPedia** is a great idea that deserves mine, his and your attention.

I am both flattered and anxious to write about **eHappyPedia**. Flattered since my idea still resonates in Dr. De Serres' imagination years after. I have to tell you that Jean is someone pretty busy too! He has no free time for trivial stuff.

You see, I met with Jean a few years ago while he was CEO of *Hema Quebec*, the equivalent of the *Red Cross* in Quebec, manufacturer and distributor of blood products and other related drugs, a big organization with tens of thousands of volunteers and 1300 employees.

We started as strategic partnership wanting to help to save human lives and improving the odds of a social cause lacking attention and love.

Sometimes at opposite ends of the table, we learned quickly to respect and to appreciate each other for the men we are, not the titles nor the functions.

On the way, we discovered common interests in the love for music, philosophy and finance. Even if we are both very busy with our daily lives, we enjoy gathering with our family and finishing the week around a friendly meal.

I am anxious since we will be writing about projections and the future. Jean wants us to write about **eHappyPedia** like I am writing about **Mdex**. The difference is that **Mdex** is real, and **eHappyPedia** is still a projection for the most part.

Sure, I've built the platform, and we have articles on, but this book is about building a company and how a mentor is going the extra miles to bring the attention and interest back into a dormant project.

Knowing Jean, I know that he has a greater idea behind his words. Actually, that's what scared me the most! Add this to my personality and signature: I walk my talks. I will be stuck doing what I will write within the next pages and chapters... or die trying.

But since I am saying **YES** to everyone, I cannot hesitate to embrace what my mentor and one of my closest friend, Jean, is asking from me. So I said **YES**.

For a whole week, I was scratching my head to find a way to start this book and write what I can vouch for. Meanwhile, I hid behind my other responsibilities until the inspiration came knocking. And it has, this morning, waking me up at dawn...

This will be a fantastic experience since it will force my mind to project even with more clarity and in parallel with my other projection,

**Mdex**. To run many projects in parallel is not a first for me. But to run two Titan projects as **Mdex** and **eHappyPedia** side by side will be a big bet.

I am not saying that I will do it. I am saying that I am open to evolve and to embrace the day as I preach in each one of my books. In my last book, **SELFMADE**, I said that I now evolve at the speed of my thoughts... Jean picked up on it. Be careful what you wish for...

With his experience and expertise as *MANAGER OF THE YEAR*, Dr. Jean De Serres will bring wisdom and body to this crazy dream called **eHappyPedia**.

He got this award for bringing efficiency and growth to a large non-profit enterprise dedicated to health. In here, that wisdom will be applied to social media dedicated to happiness.

We both believe in its potential and you will too, as soon as you understand what and why we are pushing forward. I just needed to be remembered.

For the happiness of everyone, for friendship and for the chance of a better tomorrow, here I am, naked and hopeful. Hopeful that confidence is waiting ahead.

This is **eHappyPedia, THE RISE OF THE UNICORN.**

HAPPINESS IS A
STATE OF MIND
THAT EMPOWERS
OUR BELIEFS

HAPPINESS IS THE FIRST STEP TO
CONFIDENCE
OR VICE VERSA
THAT'S THE COOL PART WITH
HAPPINESS

IT'S NOT ABOUT WORDS OR
ORDER
TRUE HAPPINESS IS
A FEELING
DEMANDING TO BE
SHARED

# CHAPTER 1

## "KNOWLEDGE IS THE GROUND FROM THE PAST"

by Dr. JEAN DE SERRES

The fun I have spending time and working with Bak is the fun of diversity and open-mindness, of happiness and wishing for a better future.

Diversity, because we go the same way with our major differences: like I needed to change his title for this paragraph right upfront. He wrote *knowledge is the ground of the past*, I immediately wanted to say **FROM** instead. Right there, a difference in the first five words!!!

And whereas differences in many circles will trigger conflict and miscommunication, anger or disappointment, here, my thoughts about my different view was immediately generating a smile. Bak and I would build upon those differences, we would bond on them instead of growing apart.

"WE USE OUR DIFFERENCES AS AN EXCUSE TO BUILD
RATHER THAN TO BEGIN AN ARGUMENT."
Dr. JEAN DE SERRES

I smiled because I know that our differences come from our backgrounds, and are more about personalities than values. Still, we both like to express ourselves, so I pushed my point for making it a bit more MINE while acknowledging that HIS giving a title to the paragraph was pushing me to write it.

We both work with this difference, we create from it. And we have fun doing so! I believe this is the recipe for great success and friendship:

"YOU BRING TWO DIFFERENT HUMANS TOGETHER
AND OUT OF THEIR DIFFERENCES, YOU CREATE!"
Dr. JEAN DE SERRES

Wow, it should be more than a management slogan, it should be a doctrine and a religion!

This recipe is so fundamentally human! It assumes that humans do better than technology. First and foremost, because they have FUN. Secondly, because what is not compatible, if they work together, will simply blow your mind!

Try using an android phone with an IOS system, try using a European power plug in an American outlet. But two different humans, wow! That's an entirely different story!

"DIVERSITY IS THE SPARK OF CREATION."
Dr. JEAN DE SERRES

So how different? Well, we're not from the same generation, me being a baby boomer and him being, well I don't know how to call his generation, it's up to him to describe it. And besides, I'm confused by the millennium, Ys, Xs, etc.

Signs of the differences? He writes his books out of his phone while I would still use a pen and paper. We're different in our approach to risk: I would never gamble while he is continuously betting on ideas and opportunities, and he calls that: to create and to embrace life.

We are also different in how we express ourselves: I calculate, I'm diplomatic, reserved and sometimes introvert. Bak is bold, extravagant and definitely extrovert. He snaps ideas like he breathes while I'm thinking about it for days, weeks and months.

He is a creative artist while I'm more of an experienced operator. But we both love music! Playing music together was how we bonded as friends. After all, it takes many different instruments to make a symphony! Those music sessions cemented our interest in each other. Fun and music!

It started with music, and then the discussion went on to business and philosophy. We are always blending our differences in knowledge, approaches and culture into creative and respectful discussions. So the differences are melted into new creations!

Dr. JEAN DE SERRES

We quickly thought this combination could make a big success: Bak and his ideas, me with management experience. So when he started talking about his new idea of **eHappy**, **eHappyPedia**, I listened. Well, this is me: I listen and I analyze! Where many would have said, this is crazy, you want to go after Facebook? On your own? Not a chance! I said: I need more details and more data.

Here, I need to stop to say that I believe in humans. Sure there are some extraordinary humans able of things that nobody else can do, like a star pianist or star football player.

But I believe that all people can come close to it. All humans can succeed!

After all, the Beatles were not the best musicians of all times, but they made it big. Mark Zuckerberg was not a seasoned social media executive before starting Facebook. So why not us?

I said to Bak: possible, but we need capital, we need a niche, opportunity and speed... and, well, good management unless we are incredibly lucky, for a long time. I believe success usually requires Luck, lots of Luck if you're thinking Big Success.

Let's not count on luck though. I'm into middle success! Reaching market and simply being a player that survives in the long term as there many definitions of a win! And Luck, we do not control. I dismiss it unless the gamble is worth the gain, with a great **X factor**.

But here, a quick search on the web led me to discover hundreds of social media, all trying to oversize Facebook. Hundreds and thousands, not dozens ! That is not even including all the startups in incubators all around the world, and all the ideas still nurtured in dreamers' minds.

There are hundreds of startup social media in the English language, thousands in Chinese, Arabic, Japanese, German or French.

Out of this overcrowding, a chance is something slim, very slim! I told you that I am not a gambler, I don't buy lottery tickets, I analyze, and I plan to win. Have you noticed, I don't play either, it is all a big waste of time if you ask me. I have fun, but I don't play!

That being said, I do take my chances when the odds are at least 50% favorable. Yes, I do gamble on opportunities I deem worthwhile. And so does Bak, but he will bet even if the odds are less than 50%. That's another key difference between our personalities. I call my gamble an investment !

So here we are, and we need capital, a niche market and management, good management. The ideas and the concepts we have. Bak already designed and set up a prototype of the web site. The next step is to assess and to test the market.

Everybody who just discovered programming think Facebook is all about programming and many who dream about creating a Facebook throw themselves to learn to program.

After all, it is labelled as a Tech company, right? But it is not, it's all about fame! It is a marketing company. And this is the market we need to know better.

How do we do this? There is the big way: to hire consultants like KPMG, Ernst & Young, Deloitte and have them do the market researches and the projections, but at a pretty fancy tag price. The tag price is reasonable for a company the size of Facebook, but not for a startup.

The web yields lots of data on the general market: it is actually billions of dollars and it will grow 5, 10 or 15% per year for the next five years. This will make some junior consultant say "your company is worth 10M$ already because it will take 10% of the world market!"

This is all crap! First, they take data from the web as cash and pure reality while it is not often accurate or complete; secondly, they assume that you are the only one in the world entering the competition, which is obviously false! Thirdly, they grab 10% of the market, based on a spreadsheet... Beautiful thinking, plain and simple. But not realistic!

Yes, the amount of data we can gather from the web is absolutely phenomenal: billions and billions of dollars. It is a colossal market, continuously growing!

Wow! Now this calls for immediate warning: if a market is that huge, the competition will also be proportional, and some competition will have infinite capital, I mean, billions of dollars. It doesn't mean they are better, but they can afford mistakes, and that's a big plus!

But competition won't have a team of creative dreamers like ours! That's our edge. With Bak writing books after books, 37 in less than 2 years, that speaks volume. That's a bet I am ready to take! And we would get back to study the competition later.

I would stress a few rules during this project:
**Rule # 1**: Study the Market, that's the easy part. Not the numbers but the processes. A few years ago, we thought Google was free but now we know they sell our information. Need to understand how competition works !

**Rule # 2**: A huge market means nothing! But investors are usually sheeps willing to bet on the past successes. Well, I mean, knowing how big it is, is easy. But the size is also what investors start the conversation with. So numbers matter!

I said it being huge meant nothing because, on one side, you could say this is great, but it also means huge competition! So what's the conclusion? We need to find gaps in the competition, customer ill-served, weaknesses in quality, in price, in presentation.

A striking conclusion is that the abundance of small size social media means there are many, many *niche* markets. There are niches for those seeking the best, the biggest, more private, the one in their language, the local ones, their Community, for those with a particular hobby, with specific equipment, those who have special interest… Name it, they all exist, out there in the vastness of the world wide web.

Bak's idea is that there is none focused on *Happiness*. He said that the happiness inspired by his son gave him the idea for **eHappyPedia**. I liked that. I like the idea, and I love the narrative.

Now, if we dive in, what is the market data showing? Is there a need or an interest in happiness? Indeed none was showing how many customers **eHappyPedia** would attract.

Keep in mind that despite all its billions in valuation, the number of Facebook followers true worth only mean one thing: its usefulness to an advertiser!

Is there an interest in *happiness*? I surely guess so. In the same period, I came onto a special Times magazine edition about *Happiness*, yes *Happiness*. That was a sign from God!

It was foremost a sign that Times magazine had done its own market survey and found interest in happiness. This was a key moment!

eHappyPedia, THE RISE OF THE UNICORN, this is the title of our book together. A Unicorn, that is really what I believe this idea of *Happiness* is, a magical and unique rare breed on its own.

This is our story and our journey together, one of hope and respect. I will be the mentor pushing his protege to new heights. I got awarded **Manager of the Year award** by improving the productivity of a public company with creativity rather than pension and jobs' cuts! My task would be to support his vision and make the dream a reality.

While Bak is busy changing the world, I will be here to remind him that his creativity is needed in every person life with the rise of eHappyPedia, the Unicorn.

The world deserves a break, an oasis of joy and the hope to break free of the circle of bad news and dramas.

This is eHappyPedia, THE RISE OF THE UNICORN.

HAPPINESS IS A
STATE OF MIND
THAT EMPOWERS
OUR BELIEFS

HAPPINESS IS THE FIRST STEP TO
CONFIDENCE
OR VICE VERSA
THAT'S THE COOL PART WITH
HAPPINESS

IT'S NOT ABOUT WORDS OR
ORDER
TRUE HAPPINESS IS
A FEELING
DEMANDING TO BE
SHARED

# CHAPTER 2
## "HOW IT ALL STARTED"

by Dr. BAK NGUYEN

Three years ago, I woke up one morning understanding that my country needed me as we were heading for the federal elections. I had no intention to run, but for freedom and country, I stepped up. I had to say what I held inside. I picked up the phone and started poking to play my part for freedom and country.

What I realized that day is: do not wait for people to ask for your help, especially when it is about country and patriotism. It is for us, as citizens, to take our place, and to serve and contribute to our society and a better tomorrow.

With that in mind, I was ready to charge! Within a few phone calls, I was sitting at influential tables where the difference is made.

I gave it my best shot. I was surprised how welcomed I was in that circle of influence and power. Don't get me wrong, people were not convinced, but facing a challenge, they always hear out the newcomer before discarding him or her. So I had my shot and most of what I predicted, happened.

Politics is all about the future. Who will win and who will have the favour of the public. How they will act and what consequence it might bring.

I shared my views with them and, by elections' night, most of my predictions were confirmed. I know, I am sorry, I cannot be more precise here, out of respect and non-disclosure agreements…

Just like when I met with Jean, I meant Dr. Jean De Serres, trying to change the game and saving lives, to play in the *big leagues* is not as hard as one might think! One simply needs to step up and to walk the talk.

It won't do you any good to look around and wait. March and people will be joining. That's what happened. We won the elections without me having to run in the frontline.

"MARCH AND PEOPLE WILL BE JOINING."
Dr. BAK NGUYEN

To face the battles and the challenges, I gathered a team to build online tools and platform to democratize and decentralize power and influences. EmotiveNow was born.

EmotiveNow is a social network and a crowdfunding platform to raise money and to give a voice to leaders, all leaders looking to empower the others and to make the world a better place. Only hate and religion were not part of the rise of the people.

"TO MAKE THE WORLD A BETTER PLACE."
Dr. BAK NGUYEN

We developed tools that took care of the heavy lifting of branding and social leveraging for causes, visions, even businesses with a significant impact on their environment and the people.

Among the tools we developed, there was a way for everyone to post a RESOLUTION explaining the problem they are trying to address, their proposed solution and to identify and connect with the people concerned about the same problem.

We opened up channels of communication between those wanting to contribute and the organizers. We worked for means to simplify and polish the presentation of the **RESOLUTION** once shared on the social networks. Those were the glams.

The real core of **EMOTIVENOW** was the crowdfunding engine we had to put in place to allow each **RESOLUTION** to gather both social support and financial weight. There were thousands of lines of code… and more.

The beta tests were running well, and the branding was a real success. We launched the branding video and a Facebook page to gather people's attention.

With a tiny small marketing budget, people were drawn to like and to see the introduction video and the post. The beta test was, in reality, more of a market research since our team were not ready to launch the site online for security concerns.

Within days, we had thousands of hits on social networks. I underestimated the time of development, and the elections were won before I had a secured version up and running.

After the elections, I can tell you that the interest in **EMOTIVENOW** lost much appeal. But I kept going, investing from my own pocket because I believed in the vision.

A few months into the project and tens of thousands spent, we had our first welcome, from Russian hackers. Within a week, we got cyber attacked and cyber sieged three times.The IPs seemed to point at Russia. I will be very careful here not to point fingers, but it was about protecting our integrity and our site.

They were desperately trying to inject lines of code. The lines of codes were mainly "poke" to test the liability of our system. After the initial attack, two more came from the same region of the world, all more intrusive and aggressive than the previous one.

What was amazing to us is that we were still in beta testing, and there wasn't any money transferred on the platform yet! Sure, it was an attack, but also a compliment to be a target at that early stage of development.

Actually, it was a blessing. After the initial surprise and shock, I summoned my team, and we had a long discussion.

By the third cyber attack, the site crashed completely. They were taking no prisoner at this stage. We had backups, but it underlined our weakness and the importance of security and encryption in this business.

The security issue is a matter of great importance, and we didn't have the means to launch a platform secured enough to withstand the storms proportional to our ambitions. It was a big disappointment, but we had to face the facts.

LIABILITY AND ASSET, TO BE SUCCESSFUL IN BUSINESS
ALWAYS KNOW WHICH IS WHICH.
Dr. BAK NGUYEN

As I met with Jean to discuss the matter, my asset was promising, but the liabilities were greater, too great! He stayed silent and listened carefully to each of my arguments.

He saw the passion in my eyes, but moreover, he recognized the leadership and the courage it took to acknowledge that we didn't have the necessary means to further push this endeavour.

Jean is a man of means, and he has the connections to raise the needed capital to jumpstart EMOTIVENOW, but we both agreed that it might take more thinking and tweaking before we could go in front of investors. What happened next surprised both of us. We were in January.

Usually, by February, I take a week off to rest and to replenish with my family. I had that liberty since my son was only 5, and he didn't miss much school.

That year, I went to the United States, where I had some business to attend. Between the meetings, I spent as much time as I could, playing and shopping with William. The Disney store was his favorite.

I remembered that after a long afternoon of business meetings, I was walking him through the mall. We finally found his favorite store. We went in, and he went nuts around the die-cast models of cars and planes.

I circled the entire store, meanwhile, he was stuck at the same spot looking at the die-cast models. I told him that he could have one, it was just for him to choose.

An hour later, or what it seems to me like an hour, he wasn't still sure of which one to pick. Tranie, his mom, was growing impatient, and I was starving. So I looked at William, and was about to tell him to hurry up.

He looked at me with those *puppy eyes*, not asking for nothing, but more time. He loved them all. He did wait the whole afternoon while I was busy dealing with my business affairs...

An idea came to my mind. "William, do you want all of them?" He didn't have to say anything, looking at his expression, I could see how I got his attention.

"You can have them all if you learn one new word for each one of them. Also, you will have to carry all of them to the cashier and back to the hotel." There were five models. He agreed on the spot.

I was looking for ways to teach him words and concepts about growing into a good man. So he had to repeat and learn:

"BE SMART, BE STRONG, BE FLEXIBLE,
BE GENEROUS AND BE KIND"
Dr. BAK NGUYEN

Those were the five words I wanted him to remember and, eventually to understand. By the time we drove back to the hotel, he was in possession of these five new words. He did not understand them yet... one step at a time.

Needless to say that I was pretty proud of my kid and of myself as a father. I love to indulge those I love, especially when they deserve it. By learning those words, it made the whole experience very productive, and Tranie was nowhere close of accusing me of spoiling my kid.

By the next morning, as we had breakfast with his grandparents, I was eager to brag about my recent success. I asked William what he learned yesterday, those five words. Coming out of his mouth were:

WILLIAM BAK

I was just too into my own world to understand what just happened. I kept asking him about those five words and eventually, they came out. But always, be happy was the first sound to resonate.

It took me a moment, but I finally realized what really happened: my son was teaching me the importance of *Life* and of being a great man by being happy first!

That kept me going for days after I understood the wisdom of my kid. By the time we got back to the office, Happiness was still resonating both in my heart and my head.

What do we do with **EMOTIVENOW**, and more importantly, what is my team focusing on next? William gave his answer: **eHappyPedia**, an online encyclopedia of recipes of happiness, a place where people can share their stories of joy, success and happiness, just for the pleasure of sharing, and of empowering one another. Well, he said be happy. I added the rest.

Most of our code and platform could be recuperated and recycled to fit **eHappyPedia**, only the branding needed to be reforged and re-articulated. It took me a month, and we were back on track.

I remembered that I didn't want to disappoint Jean with only fragments of an idea, so I stayed quiet for a month and held my head down as I was building eHappyPedia.

When we finally met, I showed him the result, like a brand new car... a new endeavour! My engineers worked around the clock to make it happened, it was still a beta prototype, but it was working, and we had no security nor liability issues.

Jean was ecstatic, he didn't know what to say at first. Within the hour, he rallied to the idea. By the time he drove home and had some time on his own, he was sold, solidly sold!

He liked the idea and spirit, but he loved even more how I tweaked things around to change a failure into a new hope. A new hope... Now we still needed to raise millions to support the dream.

"ASK AND YOU SHALL RECEIVE!"

It wasn't a FACEBOOK kind of success yet, but it was the biggest I've achieved in terms of reach and popularity until that point. One by one, people started to respond and started sharing their thoughts and recipes of happiness.

We had to support the launch through Facebook marketing. People were responding, but it wasn't a viral success. People were curious, but for every 40 readers, we had one writer. At least, the site was secured and didn't attract the same kind of attacks than EMOTIVENOW.

Within the first three months, I personally read each of the posts, thousands of them. If I wanted to understand what is Happiness to the people, it was eye-opening and empowering. I started sharing my own recipes too.

I became pretty good at sharing my thoughts, even a little addicted. My readership rose, and more and more people were interested in the new concept.

That's how I kept my morale up, feeding on the dent we successfully made in the social canvas. Our presentation and concept were a success! We were attracting people from social networks to click and open the links to our articles and website. That was a big win!

It was pretty cool to see the words taking shape into a text. Within the logarithm of **eHappyPedia**, you choose a category, and a few keywords to sort and identify your text, and it is ready to be published on social networks, mainly Facebook and LinkedIn.

Texts of **eHappyPedia** look amazing from the social networks. They look like they are straight out of a magazine, a specialized magazine dedicated to the different "branches" of happiness.

Success, Food, Travel, Friendship, Love, name it, it is there, custom-fitted to your intend, with style and ease. That, we managed to achieve flawlessly.

It was a great relief after the failure of its predecessor, **EMOTIVENOW**. The "e" of **eHappyPedia** was there to remind us of what we learned from our previous experience.

Dr. BAK NGUYEN

What wasn't as successful is that we failed to inspire people to write and share their thoughts and recipes. I was generating readers, but I needed them to write, and that was the problem.

The standard ratio is often 1 producer for any 20 consumers. We were far behind. To keep pushing forward with facebook ads to attract writers made no business sense, nor was it sustainable for a long time.

So we designed new ways to "*reward*" and empower our writers. After the publishing tools, I asked my chief engineer to wrap his mind around the **AUTHOR CORE** and the **TRIBUTE CORE**. A logarithm that allowed each text to be attributed to its authors.

Of course, each post has a number of views, just like **YOU TUBE**, but we went further, cumulating the sum of the views of all the text of a specific Author to give him or her his social weight on the web. We called it his Influence Index.

At the time of this writing, my **Influence Index** was 185 701. That means that my posts on **eHappyPedia** had been opened 185 701 times. That speaks volume.

The **TRIBUTE CORE** is a way to dedicate a text to someone. Again, the number of views of all the texts dedicated to someone is summed up in the **Fame Index**. At the time, my Fame Index was 81 434.

Those are tools and ways to *gamify* the writing and sharing process. Their main objectives are to empower the creative spark in each of us, giving it recognition and social weight.

**eHappyPedia** became more than a simple project or a business endeavour to me, it was the space and the opportunity to dialogue with an audience.

Having read all the posts, I created different tags and "magazines" in response to the type of texts that I was reading. We were still struggling to find people to actively to generate content.

The public came into our website, but only if we had new and fresh content. With our improvements and designs, the publishing tools were proven to be great and appealing to businesses and different organizations.

Later on, I had a few talks with some city's officials as they were telling me that they needed a place to have citizens share their stories in the context of Montreal's 375th. Eventually, the idea of supporting Canada's 150th surfaced on the table too.

I put my team to the task, and we custom fit **eHappyPedia** for both those national events. We were ready, but the officials were not as enthusiastic as we had hoped. It was finally a misfire. But we had pushed **eHappyPedia** to the next level.

With governments and big organizations, the dynamic is different. People like to discuss and to plan. I am a little different: by the time it took me to write a proposal, I had the prototype up and running. I am at my core, an entrepreneur and a disruptor.

In the business world, that kind of speed and enthusiasm made my success. In the governmental world, I got lost. I know that I had a great product and a way to leverage over something even greater.

Can you imagine that I even had a Bank's Vice-President to vouch for a sponsorship of a quarter-million if the Federal government was moving forward… (I am not free here to disclose the details).

But with governments, it is about forms and waiting in line. Talks and talks and plans. I know that I could have pushed more and been more patient, but I lost interest. I simply lost interest. I am not someone who will stand in line waiting. I moved on and found other means to my invention.

A few months later, I even used **eHappyPedia** to jumpstart my career as a writer. Looking to gain momentum and to keep up my writing, I first posted some chapters of my first books on **eHappyPedia**. That's how I managed to have such an **Influence Index**.

What really happened is that my attention had to be diverted back to my dental company, **Mdex & Co**, for the launch of the new business model in dentistry.

I was looking for ways to communicate my idea and vision without paying a fortune to have the salespeople selling a dream.

That's when I had the opportunity to go on stage and start sharing my vision and journey. I got prepared to speak in front of a big crowd. I started writing my speech within chapters, one chapter at a time, telling my journey as an entrepreneur.

The **Influence Index** kept me going and empowered the newly found confidence I had as a writer. Thirty-seven books later, I owe my writing career to a platform and a tool that I created to share happiness.

This is what I made out of **eHappyPedia**. But **eHappyPedia** is much more powerful. It can allow anyone to create his or her own publication and digital magazine within minutes, to give a voice to each with style, elegant designs and ease. But we ran out of money...

I had **Mdex & Co** to launch. **EMOTIVENOW** was the first chapter. **eHappyPedia** was the second. I was moving on to the third: *World Record Writing Author*. Until Jean wanted to make a "stand-alone" of **eHappyPedia**.

It has its merits and deserved its own book, he said. **eHappyPedia** is more than a single chapter in my life, according to him. He used his influence and friendship to convince me to give it another try, a second life.

**THE RISE OF THE UNICORN**, that's how this book came to life. Because Dr. Jean De Serres refused to let a great idea fade away slowly.

**eHappyPedia** is that, a *Unicorn* that needs our love and attention to flourish and grow into the Pegasus that it is destined to become. Just like it gave me support and my wings back, it is time for me to return the favor.

Too many great destinies are at stakes for us to drop the ball now. If **eHappyPedia** helped me to launch my career as an author while I was still an insecure writer looking for footing, it has the power to empower all the dormant geniuses of the world.

Genius or not, we all need a place to better share and to rejoice. Enough of the negativity and the culture of fear, we all have the right to happiness. This our chance for empowerment, for connections, for friendship.

I will come back at the drawing table, and on the construction field because I care, because Jean cares, because we have faith in a better tomorrow, for all of us.

If everyone is happier, the whole world will vibrate differently. And from there, we can build a world far better than the one we have inherited.

This is **eHappyPedia, THE RISE OF THE UNICORN.**

HAPPINESS IS A
STATE OF MIND
THAT EMPOWERS
OUR BELIEFS

HAPPINESS IS THE FIRST STEP TO
CONFIDENCE
OR VICE VERSA
THAT'S THE COOL PART WITH
HAPPINESS

IT'S NOT ABOUT WORDS OR
ORDER
TRUE HAPPINESS IS
A FEELING
DEMANDING TO BE
SHARED

# CHAPTER 3
## "THE BUSINESS PLAN"

### by Dr. JEAN DE SERRES

We did not have time to start implanting one idea that Bak has already launched a new one: the ELECTIONS. Three elections were coming up, and he thought that political parties could use **eHappyPedia** as a platform to recruit volunteers, raise money and communicate with their crowd. This would be the most significant marketing coup ever!

I froze for a moment. Ok, new plan, maybe good, maybe bad. Ambitious, but by now, I'm used to this with my friend, Bak. Too ambitious? Ok, perfect timing, opportunistic.

I always wanted to have a voice in election times, why not now? But one of those elections was the United States of America. Wait a minute… could we be accused of international interference? That's a Hollywood scenario that we do not want, one that we do not need.

We could be hacked by one party and be at the center of an international scandal! What a scoop! And a lawsuit…We were getting too much into  the House of Cards kind of stuff.

The Canadian elections seemed a better fit: we're offering a free platform to help recruit volunteers eager to participate in different ways to the democratic system. Always with the idea of a better world and under the theme of happiness.

Bak was also telling me about the **AUTHOR'S CORE**, the **FAME INDEX**? I didn't understand the concept right away, but I thought: I would like to write a few paragraphs on **eHappyPedia** myself.

I used to write editorials for a medical magazine called **L'OMNIPRATICIEN**. I ended up doing so because I was the medical editor for this new magazine that quickly rose to become the second most popular medical magazine in the Quebec medical community.

I was in charge of finding medical writers and heading the review committee as much as developing a vision for the publication. I initiated a partnership with the Quebec College of Family Physicians, which gave us credibility and a team of reviewers.

I started some new and original series of articles, and I recruited all the writers, including the most famous teacher at the time at McGill according to medical students (I was listening to them and surveying them !), someone who rose to become a real superstar in medical writing later on, but still unknown at the time.

The success was such that the magazine was bought by **L'Actualité Médicale**, the number 1 competitor, and our medical section replaced their original section.

Looking back on it, I must say that I am saddened that everyone thought it happened by itself. I never got the recognition from those who followed me and inherited the vision, the authors and the original series.

I took the opportunity to speak up for things no one was talking about. Either because of some *omerta* (law of silence), but much more often because of ignorance. Sometimes, because no one ever put together all the pieces of the drama, or no one challenged the common myths. It was a series of editorial off-trends.

Now, I was out of medicine, but I was off-trending again. Happiness seemed to be "off-trend" to me.

At school, for example, the vast majority of novels and stories that are mandatory readings are about suicide, depression, disappointed immigration and rape.

I found it hypocritical and stupid that a system which pretends to work to prevent dropping out and depression, is selecting the darkest stories as learning tools. 3 out of 4 stories read by my son from his high school program ended with a suicide, drowning or rape! None on creativity or success !

In our society, most manifestations are shows of anger and protest against the worst in the world! About the planet soon ending! About catastrophes!

Look at Donald Trump's elections! Look at Les carrés rouges in Quebec, at Les gilets Jaunes in France! Mostly about getting less tax or more salary or more pension, a lot about not accepting change, but not much about stopping violence, war, crime and abuse, not much about CREATING a better world!

Sometimes, it starts with a good reason, but too often, it ends up swallowing anger and violence and unilateralism!

Critics simply hate movies with happy endings ! Happiness is dull ! Why, you say you want Peace, Ecofriendliness, Solidarity but you are distracting yourselves with violence ? So Disney's are not high on their list! They much prefer the dramas. Where the villains have muscle bigger than ever, always growing bigger and stronger! Forget a Batman that looks human, it's now machine or the movie will be a flop.

The new generations use extreme words so easily: we're abused (when they don't have what they want), the planet is dying (when it's evolving, even negatively).

"NOWADAYS, IT'S PRETTY MUCH A CULTURE OF FEAR AND OF EXTREMES."
Dr. JEAN DE SERRES

You see people who fled wars, misery and death. Then you see the complaints about not getting everything, right away! As if peace, safety, food and lodging are granted from now on. As if access to luxury and equal chances was a genuine reason to do a strike or break windows and cars.

"THE ENTITLEMENT MENTALITY IS THE
TRAP OF OUR MODERN WORLD."
Dr. JEAN DE SERRES

We rarely see celebrations of happiness, of gratitude: but we live in a society in which everyone can walk outside and feel safe, where anyone has access to education and healthcare.

Not to say that this is perfect ! Not to say that some people have serious problems, but as a society, there are many things going well! We achieved much since the wars and the dinosaurs. And who is celebrating the successes, the progress, the happiness?

"A GLASS HALF FULL, A GLASS HALF EMPTY,
WHO IS CELEBRATING THE GLASS HALF FULL?"
Dr. JEAN DE SERRES

I want to share the idea
That being outside and safe in a green area
Is a great happiness?

That cooking a wonderful meal
Is happiness
That with our kids any deal
Is a great happiness

That center to Bak's and my life
There is the love with our wives
Which is pure happiness!
So there comes eHappyPedia!

So many reasons come to mind to write about happiness: minus the stupid but true reasons like having a great cafe latte in the morning, or the touch of great clothing bought cheaply at Costco! No need for expensive gears… or the jog in the park with mist creating a magical atmosphere! Or this romantic movie, or the music that rhymes your mind! Happy, happy, happy…

Ok, so I need to write down something! And then, as I always do, I read the conditions: long, long text of legal words. I found out that my text will be owned forever by **eHappyPedia**! That I won't have any control over it.

Now, even when the control is under a friend, let's remember that we want to grow this company, and we will have investors who may take control of it, or that we might share control and equity with.

To me, the legal text was badly written. To read legal documents is my everyday job, although I am no lawyer. It may come as service done in a friendly manner, but when lawyers want to do things simply, they write in this "*extreme*" style, overprotective for their client, but just not respectful in my opinion for the partners. I'm a fan of Kenneth Adams movement to write in modern and clear legal language! And in Fair language too!

The conditions allowed **eHappyPedia** to do whatever it wants with your text, post it out of context, maybe still attached with the author's name, especially if the author is a rising star. Happiness is also empowerment! And this was not!

Not acceptable to me. I told Bak about it. It would not be an easy job to respect the authors, help them grow without losing them if they hit fame and still protect the company: because we also needed to protect the company.

What for? First, in case **eHappyPedia** makes someone famous and that this new star-partner would move its recently famous creation elsewhere after the fame! What about our investment in advertising which would have been central to this new fame?

What about the help provided by our brand name **eHappyPedia** in order to reach stardom? Also, who pays to remove the creations from the site! **eHappyPedia** needed some rights, although not all the rights.

I had a few ideas on how to give some rights back in the eventuality of success! But the lawyers could not help much. First, they were volunteers and not motivated to spend enough time to make it right.

Secondly, we needed to think about many countries, in fact, all the countries. We ended up spending weeks rewriting the consent, and this was time taken off the project. But this was not the first time legal would slow us down.

We also needed an agreement for our partnership, a shareholder's agreement. And there was a little issue to start with: Bak had already started the company because, of course, he is a *man of action*. A company that's already got traffic is worth something.

We can simply NOT add shares without giving them some market value. And even if we give shares now, after the creation of the company, there are taxes considerations: the government would consider it a transfer of value (TOV) and would request taxes to be paid! We were seeking cash, we were not in a position to bleed cash to the government from the start!

Well, we didn't want to spend first on taxes, especially at this stage! An advice to all, if you start a new company, think about taxes upfront, right away.

Besides, since the company would not be 50 - 50, what split was adequate? It's always a picky issue between friends. Bak offered 20%, and I felt it was fair: he came up with the basic idea, and he made the first investment, so he deserved a bigger share.

My role was to bring in management, credibility with investors, friendship, and some ideas. So we settled for 25%. But because of taxes, it still needed to be 25% of 0, not of something!

So we needed the company to be a real start-up with no asset. The solution was that **Mdex** owned the concept **eHappyPedia** and had paid for the early investment, and they would simply sell the rights of **eHappyPedia** for future revenues.

Bak and I would start **eHappyPedia**, an empty shell which would, as its first step, license the concept from **Mdex**. Then, the value was to be created AFTER the creation of the company.

And for this, we needed the other piece of Legal: the shareholders' agreement. Of course, it's easy to find templates of this legal document that states the rights of each shareholder: who can buy or sell more shares, how decision are taken, what needs to be shared, what happens in case of death, divorce, bankruptcy…

Locally, there is an association of Angel Investors that specializes in start-ups: we took their basic shareholder's agreement and spent hours adjusting it for our special case.

There again, the friendship could be strained: the shareholders' agreement gives some veto rights and some common obligation, but the majority owners still control the company. Legal protection cannot replace the good choice of partners!

In some cases, the majority lacks respect for the minority. In other cases, the minority blocks everything, and it's called a toxic investor.

"A BUSINESS IS A COMMON PROJECT:
YOU PLAY AS A TEAM AND YOU DIE AS A TEAM"
Dr. JEAN DE SERRES

I believed in this project, in the need of the world to have a culture of happiness and gratitude. I really wanted this to work. In order to make a better tomorrow and the world a better place, we needed to do our homework first. Legal and fiscal homework.

This is **eHappyPedia, THE RISE OF THE UNICORN.**

HAPPINESS IS A
STATE OF MIND
THAT EMPOWERS
OUR BELIEFS

HAPPINESS IS THE FIRST STEP TO
CONFIDENCE
OR VICE VERSA
THAT'S THE COOL PART WITH
HAPPINESS

IT'S NOT ABOUT WORDS OR
ORDER
TRUE HAPPINESS IS
A FEELING
DEMANDING TO BE
SHARED

# CHAPTER 4
## "ON THE FIELD"

by Dr. BAK NGUYEN

Here comes the beginning of the hard part, the work on the field. Three years ago, I started the first draft of **eHappyPedia**. We launched it on Facebook, targeting the university's students. The response was pretty encouraging. We had about 1000 entries within weeks.

People were invited to share a happy anecdote or a recipe of success. Some wrote more than others and some, only a few words. We were not judging, everyone was welcomed to join.

Pretty quickly, the texts came in, in both languages, French and English. So we had to sort out the different tongues. As I was planning with my engineers, we decided to extend **eHappyPedia** to the eight most talked tongues on the internet, based on a Google search.

English - French - Spanish - Hindi - Chinese - Japanese - Russian - Portuguese were the official languages of **eHappyPedia** version 1.

It was more than just a matter of programming, we needed to brand promotional videos in each of those languages to support the launch of the site.

Within three months, our videos accumulated more than 2.5 million views on Facebook and You Tube combined. We just hit something big, really big. It hit much harder than our previous attempt with **EmotiveNow**, the legacy platform.

I went on and surfed on the wave of success. By May 2016, I received the honor of the **GRAND HOMAGE LYS DIVERSITY**. This award is usually attributed to honor a person who had contributed to further advance the cause of diversity and acceptance in our society.

It was a great surprise and honor to me. I used my moment of fame to announce the launch of **eHappyPedia** in front of an elite crowd of business people and government officials.

Actually, you have to hear this story. By the end of May, my mentor and friend, Dr. Mohamed Benkhalifa called me to tell me to check my emails: something great was coming.

I thanked him and waited a few days. The mail finally arrived, and I opened it. It said, "Congratulation for your nomination as a finalist for the **GRAND HOMAGE LYS DIVERSITY**…"

I am often spotted for those kinds of honor, but every time, I am a finalist and never win. I learned to not care much about the excitement anymore.

I remembered talking to my dad through the phone that morning, telling him how upset I was to always finish second in those kinds of competitions. You know what they say about being second? You are the first loser!

That day, my dad was kind enough to support me. "At least you are one of the people nominated. Those circles don't even know that I exist!" And he was right. He worked all his life and often harder than me… what right did I have to complain about my situation?

"BE GRACIOUS, BE GRATEFUL AND DO NOT HAVE ANY EXPECTATIONS BUT THOSE YOU PUT UPON YOURSELF."

**Dr. BAK NGUYEN**

So I ended up thanking him and decided to go on with my day. Yes, I had a big clinical day ahead. Usually, I am seeing 30-40 patients a day, so, I had no time to spare for trivial stuff. Let's be grateful and graceful about this nomination.

After a tremendous clinical day, I went home earlier, and I decided to stop at my parents' house to say hello. I sat down with my mom and wanted her to be proud. So I reached for my phone and opened the nomination letter.

I know, it is just a nomination, but I still can make her proud. To my surprise, she read the whole letter. At the bottom, she even opened the attachment. The first page was saying congratulation for the nomination… From the screen of an iPhone, that's all we could see.

She scrolled down and changed her expression. "Son, I think that you've won something!" That was not possible, Tranie and I both read the mail about the nomination…

I took the phone and read the letter again, but this time, I went through all the pages of the attachment. She was right!

I understood it as I reached the line saying that my presence was mandatory since I am the recipient of the Award **GRAND HOMAGE LYS DIVERSITY 2016**. I had to confirm my attendance.

I read it twice, and it was all true. Then, I panicked! The event was the next day, and I had a day fully scheduled with patients! I called my staff and cancel half of my clinical day. I also had to go online and to search for diversity. I didn't know what it meant!!!

On YouTube, most of the past winners were all people of great stature and fame talking about society and freedom… That's not my thing! I looked at myself and wondered:

And that's how it started. I wrote my thank you speech based on my understanding of diversity: not me!

The next day, I went to the event with my wife Tranie and my right-hand woman, Sana Joulid. We were open and amazed at the same time. My award was the second to last to be attributed since it was among the biggest… so many people went on to give their speeches before me.

Each time a minister or a dignitary talked, I finished a full glass of wine. I hate wine, but it was much needed since I didn't want to speak after those people. I didn't feel at ease and comfortable. Well, I was intimidated.

By the time it was my turn, there were still around 500 people in the crowd looking up at me. I didn't care. The wine was already getting to my head. I pulled my speech out and read it.

I do not recall much of the event, but I've been told that I spoke very slowly and everyone could understand each and every one of my words. You see, usually, I speak at a pretty fast pace, some times, way too fast.

In that speech, I announced that with great power comes great responsibilities. I thanked the people for their trust and said that it was now my turn to contribute with the launch of **eHappyPedia**, the encyclopedia of happiness.

"HAPPINESS IS EVERYTHING!"
eHappyPedia

The next day, I woke up and went down into the living room to see the award. It was real, I did not dream of it. I looked at the video of my speech… it was awful! I was drunk, functional, but half gone.

But still, the speech was a great one. I decided to get an actor to record my speech and had a video made on the subject. I put the video on Facebook and YouTube. Over a week, I had more than half a million views!

People were writing to me and commenting from all around the planet! This is it! This can work! **eHappyPedia** is not a dream, it is a need!

I was pretty convinced already, but just in case that I still had an ounce of doubt, I received, out of nowhere, an invite from Raymond Desmarteaux, a journalist at **Radio-Canada International** asking me for an interview.

This was both exciting and mind-blowing! A week ago, I launched an initiative and a pilot, and now I was about to be interviewed over the radio by the national broadcaster! I embraced the opportunity and gave it my best shot!

After the radio interview, posts and texts started to come in, by the dozens. I read every single one of them and started reacting to them. I intended to fix the misspelling, but soon enough, I realized that happiness could be broken down into categories. That's precisely what I did. I started designing the different categories.

I designed the categories and started planning the feel and the branding of each of them. LOVE, FRIENDSHIP, SUCCESS, TRAVEL, FOOD, LEADERSHIP... I gave to each category the same attention one would give to a brand of a distinct magazine.

Over the next few weeks, we had developed 19 different magazines of Happiness! My engineers weren't too happy about it, but it was my call. Each brand had its own design and feel. I was pretty proud of myself.

Among the tools developed, I pushed for the automating the design of texts so the looks would be as if they were straight out of a magazine. Of course, people would still need to format the sentences and the paragraphs, but the rest was ready, as an automated template.

As soon as someone finishes a text, they can *"categorize"* it in the right magazine of happiness, and within the push of a button, they are ready to share their "article" on the social networks; namely, Facebook, LinkedIn, Twitter...

That's where the magic really happened: on the social network, the cover pages and the posts are automatically generated to make sure that the articles look straight out of a magazine, one of happiness tailored to your chosen category (leadership, success, travel, love, friendship...).

With words only, it doesn't sound as powerful as it is really, but with the **eHappy** logo, it was looking great! Try it to understand the feeling both the author and the readers will feel as he or she sees his or her work published!

This is what it is, to publish your work within a branded publication, to have a voice and to take your place in the world. It is about us and us. No "I", without us!

On top of it, texts are means to tell a story, but they are also the beginning of the ramifications of references, in other words, links. So we developed tools allowing links between texts and individuals. We call those "**cores**".

Within **eHappyPedia**, there are two main cores: the **AUTHOR'S CORE** allowing a writer to compile the total views of all the texts he/she has written; and the **TRIBUTE'S CORE**, allowing texts to be dedicated to a person or a company. The **TRIBUTE'S CORE** functions as a counter of the total number of views of text dedicated to a person.

The main difference between both cores is that the **AUTHOR'S CORE** is within the control of the writer while the **TRIBUTE'S CORE** is within the control of the WEB, of ALL the writers referring to him or her.

To wrap the whole of this logic, the **AUTHOR'S CORE** gives an **INDEX OF INFLUENCE**, and the **TRIBUTE'S CORE** give an **INDEX OF FAME**. Those are metrics and social measurements we put in place, to *gamify* and keep a record of the activity of our authors.

In a word, we designed a system that is providing a voice to everyone within the constraints of happiness (respect and peace) and within the means of the web (access through a smartphone or a computer).

The implantation of the **eHappyPedia's** cores, the Author core and the Tribute core were exhilarating! I saw people reacting live to my decisions and to my structures. Talk about some social acknowledgement.

At last, the texts were coming in, but now were more and more specific and tailored to a kind of happiness, to a brand of **eHappyPedia**, of happiness.Throughout that summer, we got people filling up the forms and submitting their views of happiness.

The views were pretty good too! As soon as a post was submitted, it was shared on the social networks like Facebook and LinkedIn. Some post reached more than 2000 views within that summer! Two thousand views for a text, not a video! That was something heavy!

The more I reacted to the people, the more posts were coming in. And the crazy part was that I was managing the whole platform from my iPhone 5, with that tiny little screen! For everything I needed, my engineers pushed their ingenuity to have something functional within a week or less.

After a summer of beta testing the platform, we had achieved a great "editing and writing machine" to empower people to write. Actually, it was so easy to publish a great looking text that it enabled writers to keep posting more and more.

I joined in the frenzy as I contributed to the effort by publishing myself. Post after post. Read after read, I built up interest and a social presence. Not showing my body, but showing my mind and my soul to the people, to the world. Something magical happened, I changed somehow inside.

Maybe A WAY, not just THE WAY, to grow. Based on my personal experience, it has been the easiest and fastest way to grow and to evolve. And may I add, the least painful way that I have experienced so far.

By sharing my experiences, my ideas and my conclusions, I gave my thoughts a body and an audience starting with one: me! I quickly became my first FAN.

I know, it sounds pretty narcissistic, but it was true. You see, I am a sensitive soul and an artist at heart. *Conformity* and my parents forged a doctor out of me from fire and passion. I went on with their WILL and succeeded as such.

The process was a long and painful one for everyone walking through the steps. Believe me, there are many, many steps. Some days, it felt like a never-ending march.

I learned to keep my head down to avoid the unnecessary storms and managed to leverage on my laziness by getting out of the requirement with minimum time and effort from my part.

I've always been a very verbal person, but my formal education and my cultural background balanced my outspoken personality. If my emotions were bursting out at the beginning, I soon learned from my laziness to get on quietly and undetected.

That's how I survived dental school. Don't get me wrong, I wasn't a quiet mind, I was just wise enough not to make unnecessary noise where it wasn't welcomed. I kept my head down at school while I led as a movie producer and later on, directing the film.

That balance was surely exhausting, but it helped me cope with my studies and the painful journey of *Conformity*. From the time I spent in dental school, I grew stronger and stronger, surfing on my classes and building my character.

The strangest of thing happened when I graduated. I missed the environment of *Conformity* I despited so much. Not the first few months, but quickly enough, I missed the empowerment and the structure Conformity gave me.

At first, I thought that it was the structure that I was missing, the idea to have something to beat. The existence of an average to compare myself to, and to race against. Now that I've graduated, I had no more average to compete against.

I never fell into the trap of comparing myself to an individual to cope with my new reality, but the temptation was surely present and strong. I kept growing comparing myself to the reflection I see from the mirror, loving, hating and racing that reflection of the past and of my hope.

I evolved, I succeeded, but I wasn't happy. It took me years later to understand that I wasn't whole, that's why I wasn't happy. This is deep down, from the surface, I was among the most loved dentist, the smiling dentist... but deep down, I was miserable.

That's who I came to grow into, as a dentist, as a company. I wrote in one of my previous book that I wasn't looking to treat the teeth, but the people.

My patients helped me cope with my deception of being a dentist and the hard choice I had to make to turn my back on a possible future as a Hollywood producer.

By being warm and generous with the people under my care, I felt a calling, a purpose, or so I thought. I felt better, and I made myself useful, available.

That's really what happened the day I accepted to embrace reality, my reality of being part of *Conformity*, and the choice of my destiny not breaking free from my roots and my chains.

Against all the odds and my own beliefs, I grew into a good man and a great dentist, a kind one. One people are running to, and love. That love helped me heal or at least, cope with my days, one by one.

I went on to make **Mdex**, my dental company, into a philosophy of life and people responded well to it, from the dental chair. Now that I think of it, what I did was to recreate a community with whom to share.

I draw my strengths from the empowerment of the people, and the austerity of the dental chair gave us the means to rally to, something to beat.

In a word, I put back in the mix the ingredients that made my previous success from my old days, from school, where I was happy! I never thought that I would ever write these words. I thought I was miserable at school, I was even more after graduation.

THROUGH STRUCTURE AND WITH A COMMUNITY,
I FOUND BOTH SUCCESS AND HAPPINESS.

Dr. BAK NGUYEN

Now, years later, this is what I realize as I was building **eHappyPedia**: it is to give people a structure to beat and a chance to find a community to cope with. Aren't we all looking for happiness, and our purpose in this life?

That's how I came to leverage on my liability and my reality: to build a structure to beat. From it, came my success. From the online presence and the social recognition having people commenting and reacting to my posts, I found a community to share with.

The number of reads and the **Influence Index**, those were just numbers, but they empowered me to share more and regularly. And I grew as I shared.

This is not a beautiful story, one I made up to capture your attention. It is merely the beginning...

A year went by. As I reduced the marketing budget and the recruitment of people writing simply because I couldn't find a sustainable economic model to keep growing the community, I lost Momentum and faith in my own creation, in **eHappyPedia**.

I did not give up, I kept publishing, but I ceased to act as the father of the platform. That is to face reality. In the meantime, **Mdex & Co** was rising, fast.

Funny thing, I brought back that idea of happiness to the heart of my dental company and professional career. The new economic model of dentistry that I am proposing is one based on the quest of happiness of each dentist. I wasn't that far away from my philosophy and core of **eHappyPedia**...

Actually, I transposed the idea of happiness into a form where I had more financial leverage and influence. As I needed a mean to communicate my vision and to convince my peer dentists to join. I started taking the stage and writing books.

When all was new and endearing to me, I coped once again with my community, sharing my thoughts on **eHappyPedia**. My first chapters from

**Symphony of Skills** were posted on eHappyPedia as articles and posts of happiness, of recipes of success.

The views and the comments helped me write the next chapter, and the next one, and the next one until I drafted my conclusion.

eHappyPedia and its community held my hand and guided me through the writing of my first book, and my third and my fourth. That's how I built my **Momentum** as a writer. All from my phone!

It wasn't just the numbers of views, the automated editing was a great empowerment too. It looked nice the minute I finished writing. As I started sharing on the social network, my chapters looked polished, straight out of a magazine.

A quick win, even small. From that win, I went on to build the next one, and so on, and so on.

Two weeks, three at the most, that's the average time it will take me to compile a book, one chapter at a time, one or two happy posts a day. **Momentum**, creativity and happiness. Thank you, eHappyPedia.

Thirty-seven books later, I was holding multiple world records as an author, records to be confirmed and acknowledged, but I did it, that, no one can take away from me.

Because of the author rights and to protect my books, I stopped publishing them on eHappyPedia. Amazon and iTunes slowly replaced the encyclopedia of happiness.

I never realized until now the power that eHappyPedia gave me as I started, as I was alone, as I was unsecure. It was now time to give back, to empower back what made me.

Jean was absolutely right, I must redirect my attention and my interest in eHappyPedia and its development.

For that, I thank him. On that, I wanted to follow his lead. The proof of concept and the beta testing were complete. The market research and the incubation time were favorable and ready.

Now was the time for great management and financial empowerment to raise the needed resource for the growth of the **ENCYCLOPEDIA OF HAPPINESS**.

Not just for our sake, but to give the tools and the means to everyone and anyone to have a chance to happiness and success as it did for me.

This is eHappyPedia, THE RISE OF THE UNICORN.

HAPPINESS IS A
STATE OF MIND
THAT EMPOWERS
OUR BELIEFS

HAPPINESS IS THE FIRST STEP TO
CONFIDENCE
OR VICE VERSA
THAT'S THE COOL PART WITH
HAPPINESS

IT'S NOT ABOUT WORDS OR
ORDER
TRUE HAPPINESS IS
A FEELING
DEMANDING TO BE
SHARED

# CHAPTER 5

## "THE CHAIN OF QUESTIONS"

by Dr. JEAN DE SERRES

Being hacked was just adding to the strains. I know nothing about programming and coding, so I asked Bak, how much will it cost to make the site safe? I forget the numbers, but I remember the feeling of the answer: way too much money! Much more than we could afford it as a startup!

It's an urban legend that everyone can start an endeavor or company from a garage. Is it really the case? If I was a University professor, I would investigate the myth.

It sounds great for marketing as it makes early adopters: crowds of hopeful who will support other startups just because they think it will be theirs turn soon or people who will buy books and take MBA courses on that premise.

We all know the story of those garage startups. The founders are usually young, somehow rebellious, and their early customers were happy NOT doing business with a huge international company! Even if the startup like Apple has become the #1 company.

To me, this garage startup story sounds like pure marketing, and to a point, even false marketing because none of those garages grew up in poor areas.

They all went up in areas where there is CAPITAL available from VCs, venture capitalist firms, those international companies that manage the big money of the world.

And exactly what do those companies bring to a startup? CAPITAL. Exactly what the rebels dislike, so let's hide it. Good marketing and great irony!

In our case, we were not born with contacts, and we were not in the land of capital. But Bak was willing to bet big time and force the capital and the market.

It might sound like a great story to bet your house on your ideas, but as a true friend, of both Bak and Tranie, I could only advise NOT to BET THE HOUSE on eHappyPedia!

This would be stupid. Actually, it would have been really stupid! Even if there are stories of cases about fortunes being made by betting the house, there are so many more stories of ruin. Besides, it does not show good risk management. Didn't we say we wanted to be excellent managers?

If you have 2 eggs, don't put them in the same nest (I'm not talking about having children and split them into separate houses…, not the same thing, LOL!). I mean, don't put your retirement in your day job!

I have friends who did that because it's easy to do when you're in a bubble: talk to the people at Nortel in its heydays, who invested all their retirement funds in Nortel and lost both their retirement plan and their job all at once!

And Nortel was the biggest act on the Canadian stock exchange… it would never fall… Nortel was growing full speed, so not something you could miss. Still, they ended losing everything!

Thousands of people lost everything! There is only few Steve Job on the other side of the balance. I really believe that capital made a big difference here, the difference between a fairy tale and an opportunity.

In short, we needed capital: to fix the site and to grow. Unlike Bak, I need to analyze and to rationalize. And betting was not the solution. If our idea was good, we would found capital!

The first thing is to determine how much is needed. The trap here is to underestimate INVOLUNTARY financial needs. We see in the news every day, companies underestimating the financial needs and their consequences: construction of bridges with extra costs of over 80% of its original budget, hospitals that cost double the initial forecast, movies going way over budget, etc.

In my opinion, this is the result of VOLUNTARY underestimation. In some other times, it is just plain incompetence. It's a well-known practice to underestimate a budget to secure the contract first and to deal with the problems later.

But when you do the exercise for yourself, you need to get the real number: DON'T FOOL YOURSELF, even if you may fool others. I'm not advocating that, but unfortunately, some do. Keep the real numbers for yourself, have them near!

I think that we didn't budget correctly for the web site and its growth. None of us had any experience doing that particular kind of project before.

None of us was coding. We didn't have a full picture of all the tasks required besides coding. We were, in fact, learning on the way. Still, there were common points with other companies I was experienced in.

I believe Bak asked his chief engineer to come up with a budget. But what about the **budget for failure**? You know, when you turn the switch on and nothing happens! It doesn't work, and you need extra money to fix the unknown problem!

When you are supposed to go live on August 1st, and it's now October, and you're still paying staff and services, but the site is not LIVE nor generating any money. You must have padding for the unexpected. That's good management. Otherwise, you go under, or you sell on the cheap!

We still ended up with a budget for coding, a budget for hosting (thanks to cloud providers like Amazon and Telus), and some vague forecasts for revenues. Forecasts are where you essentially write what you want. But your story needs to convince experts! So it has to be credible.

How do you estimate how many people will connect to your site? Well, Bak educated me: not by predicting but by buying the numbers! And that was done by paying Facebook of course! You pay a number of sites for them to refer you, or to list you in their top choices or options.

But that was adding to the budget. I started feeling like an accountant! Someone was adding the numbers in red and not seeing any good numbers in black!

Because I THOUGHT MORE TRAFFIC MEANT MORE REVENUES, but now, more traffic meant we paid Facebook MORE MONEY! That is, until you have a name! Until you get HUGE numbers of clicks! And that's before considering that more traffic also meant more bandwidth, so more expenses.

Dr. JEAN DE SERRES

This is where Bak had a key point: we need marketing he told me, and I trust him, he could do good marketing. I saw the man in action. If anything, he is a human amplifier.

Dr. JEAN DE SERRES

It is sometimes used for good; sometimes, for bad, marketing is usually seen as something bad. I hate misleading marketing, but hey, without some good marketing, even the best ideas won't stand a chance.

We were going to need a lot of good marketing to make **eHappyPedia** into the success it is destined for! I am counting on Bak for that part. Does he have training in marketing, in sales and in psychology? Well, being a dentist is not exactly the same.

Dr. JEAN DE SERRES

Bak keeps asking that question, why not? Not like me wondering "*how does it work?*" and "*what data?*" I must say that he often gets very interesting answers.

93

He sees a different angle of the behaviour, every single time. Add to that a lot of enthusiasm, good faith and creativity, and you get a start of a marketing campaign! That's Bak in a nutshell.

Does he have training in communication? Well, he made movies. And he masters the new technologies as a user and a passionate fan. So, let's assume that he is a marketer 2.0, maybe 3.0.

We are a startup. Everybody assumes roles for which we are not expertly trained in. But once, again, how do you fully train in advance for something that new, a startup? Experience helps creativity and audacity weight on the other side of the balance.

So we had our lead marketer but still needed a **core message**. Sure we had the concept: a site about happiness, where everyone goes to learn, to witness, to leave traces of happiness. But how good is it as a message?

And do we have a targeted audience? What's their language, I mean, culturally speaking. And what are the right channels? All the questions I asked Bak.

So we needed some work, and as always, it was with good food and drink (coffee), at the Mansion (Bak's house), very informal. Actually, those afternoons are what kept reinforcing our friendship.

Bak had the will, but the will was different from the marketing message. I mean, he had the drive, he wanted strongly, he was willing to put everything he had behind this project, and he believed in eHappyPedia.

My question was: what is it that we are selling? And what is it that we want the customer to pay for? We all knew that social media live from advertising and the data.

The advertising cost to the customer is attention time: the time to click on something, the time to read a view or see it pass on your screen, the time to listen to a video or audio. Customer is paying with his time!

The value is in the data gathering: personal data like name, address, birth date that one gives when registering, but also data on the likes, on their preferences and interests (collected from the search words and the pages viewed). So I was asking Bak: which data would we collect that no one else collects already? What are we bringing new to this world?

In order to brainstorm about some questions, I believed the best way is to show many or all existing options in order not to reinvent the wheel. So we gathered some encyclopedias (paper actually since it is easier to spread them around the room and on the walls) to check for statistical data.

I have lots of books on demographics, so it helped. It's also funny to see how you can put a population on a graph by age, size, color of hair, sporting habits, eaten food, books read, use of pen or pencil, political orientation, sexual orientation, religion...

Oups, this is where we thought there was something. Do those tables reflect all the thinking in the mind of the people? Sure, sex is defined by orientation, but could we go deeper in the descriptions of tastes?

Food is probably described by what is sold in groceries or restaurants, but could we go deeper in defining levels of satisfaction on the macaroni of the Monday when prepared by the father versus the mother, bought ready-made or made from scratch by granny?

You can feel where Happiness is now. Could we collect happiness, or satisfaction data on everything, your bed, your night, your meal, your spouse, your friend, your government, your car, your everything including your dreams? Could we collect data that is different from what Facebook does? The answer is yes!

Could we do this through the happiness core message? YES, YES, and YES. And now, sorry but the hard question: was that info valuable? Yes, of course. This was a different form of market analysis.

Companies spend lots of money verifying the satisfaction of their customers, for their prototype product, for the product after the sale, and even for customer service.

You certainly got those calls: were you satisfied with your last visit? Or you've seen in washrooms or in theaters the little click with a happy option or smile - green, vs the not happy option red - angry face.

We would have a repository of satisfaction surveys ready-made for every company if we could get people to register all their happy thoughts on the site.

And maybe all their frustration too! But that was complicating the message. We decided to stick to happiness but keep frustration in a very good place as a Yin and Yang piece.

That was all good, but then, we needed to learn how to collect that information. I wanted it to be ethical and transparent, which is a challenge. Bak was ok with this, but we didn't know how to do this: collecting data from postings, from registration info, from monitoring views?

If the posting was the key, then we needed to generate as many postings as possible. We needed to invest in making it easy and then, guess what, I was thinking about removing legal hurdles for the few persons who are sensitive to complicated contracts like me.

Bak agreed, we would remove legal issues. But that meant we would no longer push to create value in postings on which we had relinquished all rights! See how this market orientation has an impact on the business?

We also needed easy clicks, but not a system that we would need to pay for. Bak thought our programmers would have fun building this. We also needed an algorithm to gather the info from postings. Oups! That was more complicated.

It is easy to say AI will solve it, but buying an AI solution was not going to be cheap. Paying only for service was adding a layer of debt and making our business riskier.

I thought we had to do it the same way we had done everything so far: volunteers that would get shares of the company in exchange for their work, probably AI students who needed a project for their thesis.

I suggested that in exchange for shares, we ask for the free use of the system they would develop, but they could use in non-competing businesses for their own benefit.

Would it work only with AI analysis of the posting? I didn't know, but we had to hope for it. Of course, there would be value only when we would reach a huge size, so I was expecting this would make the company NOT profitable for many years. We were convicted to quick, long and big growth! That was the only issue.

Next was how we would SELL the data? We obviously needed someone experienced in that field, someone with access and knowledge of the buyers. Someone who would set the right price. Did we know the price of the data at that time? Not at all!

We were in for a ride, Bak and me. I knew from that friendship, we were building the future together. A better future for all of us, a place of hope and of joy.

This is **eHappyPedia, THE RISE OF THE UNICORN.**

HAPPINESS IS A

STATE OF MIND

THAT EMPOWERS

OUR BELIEFS

HAPPINESS IS THE FIRST STEP TO

CONFIDENCE

OR VICE VERSA
THAT'S THE COOL PART WITH

HAPPINESS

IT'S NOT ABOUT WORDS OR

ORDER

TRUE HAPPINESS IS

A FEELING

DEMANDING TO BE

SHARED

# CHAPTER 6
## "A BUSINESS PLAN"

by Dr. BAK NGUYEN

I was meeting with the strategic team planning for the first seed of investment round for **Mdex & Co**. We had our numbers aligned, our strategy and now, we were finalizing the wording and the narrative.

I had to rush that meeting a little because I promised a friend to attend his speaking event: Andre Chatelaine, former first vice-president the Movement Desjardins.

As I left my boardroom, I was confident and proud of what we had achieved so far. I have a great and solid vision, and now, it is broken down into numbers, ratios and timelines for investors to understand.

I always knew the narrative since that's how I started the project, with a narrative. I even wrote a book on the subject, a year prior to the business plan: **CHANGING THE WORLD FROM A DENTAL CHAIR**.

I wrote that book because Ernst & Young gave me the opportunity to present my vision to their board of judges for the **ENTREPRENEUR OF THE YEAR** award.

It may have been a little too soon back then since I didn't have any financial statement to show, only the narrative. I backed it with a book, I leveraged on my position by going all-in with what I had in hand, in my head.

I built the pilot project on two floors of a prime real estate skyscraper in the heart of downtown Montreal, investing a few millions in and creating a huge debt. But I was the only dentist having signage on the GOLDEN SQUARE MILE of Montreal, beside the Ritz Carlton, the Scotia Bank head Quarters and the top luxury brands.

That's what I had to show. I had a great narrative and a book out if it. I got the nomination, but I did not win that award. Now, people wanted me to submit again. Maybe next year... I played to win, not to participate.

Dr. BAK NGUYEN

The adventure brought my story and journey to a whole new level. Never before, a contestant has done as much as to write a book to defend his nomination. I may have lost the title, but I surely gathered much attention, on which I leveraged.

That's what I realized when I was sitting in the president's chair in my boardroom: it was a little of a *déjà vu*! The trailer was out a year ago, now, the movie is coming out!

Without that trailer, I wouldn't have interested the team of great *Generals* (that's how I refer to my mentors and top executives) around me. Without that boldness, I wouldn't have a chance to capture the interest of my mentors and the attention of investors.

I had written the first tome of the journey. The second tome was in preparation, coming out, heavy and solid! That is what Jean wanted us to do, to follow the same logic.

A year ago, it was Ernst and Young who forced my hand to launch **Mdex & Co** into a narrative, a book: **CHANGING THE WORLD FROM A DENTAL CHAIR**.

This time, it was my mentor, Dr. Jean De Serres, who leveraged on our friendship to make sure that this narrative, **eHappyPedia**, had a fighting chance.

He made sure that we keep our motivation up. He did so betting on my own momentum: let's write every step of the creation of the company, perhaps into a book?

Let's think about people who will read this many years from now. Let's make things happen as we would like to remember them, and be proud of it when we'll die. This could part of our legacy.

I have to admit that until the writing of those previous words, it wasn't that clear to me. It was all a déjà vu! But from that moment on, the plan became the book to be. Suddenly, the plan could really be a dream, and the dream was merging with reality. We had to deliver, every day, day after day.

In other words, we could say that we were putting ourselves in the public eye, and someone suggested to put all that documentation in the public domain. LIVE!

A start-up being created live, the plans live, the results live. WOW! We were into something! And then, why not public funding under the eye of the public? And the book would become both a documentary and a fiction.

Why not a teaching tool? And maybe the company could become a bench lab if we could follow the suggestions of the public and act on them, or if we could measure the impacts of each of our moves.

I loved the idea. Jean, you are a mastermind, from a league of your own!

## ENCYCLOPEDIA OF HAPPINESS.

Okay, back to the boardroom. Step one, the business plan needed deep reviewing. I met with Jean and with my freshly acquired knowledge writing the **Mdex's** investor pitch. I was more than ready to write **eHappyPedia** following Jean's vision and experience.

This time, it was not about reproducing the past (**Mdex**), but about writing the future (**eHappyPedia**).

The company would become a multi-tool! A social media, an encyclopedia about happiness, a documentary with books and videos, a teaching tool, how to start a company, how to succeed (hopefully, otherwise, how to fail and what to learn on the way), but even more, a spiritual book about how to build your life!

While doing so, I would also have to compete with **Mdex**. Jean was worried about that conflict of interest: would I have enough energy for **eHappyPedia**?

**eHappyPedia** was not the only competitor of **Mdex**. My brain was exploding with ideas: books, businesses, videos, inventions and patents. I had those ideas for better tools in dentistry and better designed dental clinics.

I had a dozen books and conferences in my head. Most of all, at the time, I was experimenting with **UAX, Ultimate Audio Experience**, a new way to produce and to consume audiobooks.

I was working on my first release with director Justin Morganstein. Yes, you're right, the first release: **CHANGING THE WORLD FROM A DENTAL CHAIR**.

It was aimed to be released on iTune, Amazon and Spotify by that Fall. So would **eHappyPedia**! And in a much shorter time, since we would have the experience and templates.

I was wondering if Jean was ready for this? This was not only a book, but it was also an adventure and a journey into the world of the imagination and to Hollywood… Bak's version. And I could see the synergy with Jean's vision about writing the future while creating **eHappyPedia**!

It was a great and exciting experience, but knowing my team and my prospect investors, they weren't that open to share the details on live video. And I agreed with them.

But **eHappyPedia**? What about having the world contributing? Jean is the only person I needed to convince other than myself. I had thousands of ideas, but they were also all interrelated!

This is **eHappyPedia, THE RISE OF THE UNICORN.** Are you ready for a better tomorrow?

HAPPINESS IS A
STATE OF MIND
THAT EMPOWERS
OUR BELIEFS

HAPPINESS IS THE FIRST STEP TO
CONFIDENCE
OR VICE VERSA
THAT'S THE COOL PART WITH
HAPPINESS

IT'S NOT ABOUT WORDS OR
ORDER
TRUE HAPPINESS IS
A FEELING
DEMANDING TO BE
SHARED

# CHAPTER 7

"EXECUTION IS EVERYTHING!"

by Dr. JEAN DE SERRES

We went back to the Boardroom! In reality, there was no Boardroom where we were meeting. The one at **Mdex** was downtown and too far for me. And boards were not on working days, always on week-ends!

We were meeting in living rooms, the kitchen, or by the swimming pool! No one was paid, and it was all leisure activity if anything. But also genuine friendship!

You see, there are 2 kinds of startups: those started by employees from their current jobs, or paid by investors, and those started out of nothing like a hobby! **eHappy** was the second type. And big ideas are always a threat in that case. Because if no one is paid, if no one has to stand the other in order to keep its job, then we cannot afford significant disagreement!

The concept behind **eHappyPedia** was great but still had no major investment. The idea of writing our plan, and a testimony to the execution and making everything LIVE was not only great, but it was also the financial solution.

If people saw what we were trying to create, if we started having a few followers, a bond would be created: we would be their team, and they will invest, even better, they would go check the website and create traffic.

All we needed was a marketing coup to create awareness: I relied on Bak for that. And maybe its other books and conference were the right platform to create our buzz, the buzz.

In fact, we needed something else. I was worried we would lack breath and would not be able to follow the crowds if they were coming. We needed plans to increase our capacity, and we discussed that with our programmers.

I did need an increase right away, but I needed everything ready to increase on a snap: knowing who to call, knowing changes we would have to make.

We also needed to be a few days in advance. Yeah, it may sound like cheating, but I believed in steadiness and wanted us to be able to post something every day, every single day. We had to be 2-3 days in advance to reality.

In the Business Plan, I called those contingencies. And contingencies would not be made public. I was hoping no one would question, and I would end up being right. But contingency was the pre-work we would constantly make. It would help us big time.

I proposed a few principles:

1. Plan and Execute; make the plan public and make the results public.
2. Cut every action to the simplest task, with just one person responsible for it, and as short as possible. This would be a project management public course.

3. Link every action to a part of the plan and measure the progress of this plan in %. These would be measured by different units, sometimes money, but also time, value, completion.

4. Have a few, not too many, measures of impact on the scorecard and have it all fit on one page. Units would be traffic, money spent, the value of the company in USD (measured as an aggregate of comparable to market, of the value of traffic or assets, etc.), lights (green or yellow or red) about progress according to the plan.

5. We would have an easy, one-click option on our website to donate or become an investor. For that option to be practical, we decided to create a new company, of which **Mdex** would own 51% of voting shares, and rest was for employees and public. But the company would still be private, nothing on the stock exchange for now, too expensive and too complicated.

6. The site would have a daily post on plan and results: Bak and I would take turns every day for posting new stuff. We would look for partners to join us in this role.

7. The site would, of course, link directly to **eHappyPedia** website (and **Mdex**).

Then, of course, Bak would make a book out of those daily posts, and he would start working on a video too. I would use my contacts to get a university affiliation to make it a bench lab for starting a new company.

My friends at UQAM liked the idea. This was publicity for them, and they were growing their on-line affiliates! I asked them to get a teacher to comment every day if possible or every week on our plan and progress. One professor accepted to use her MBA class to issue comments and suggestions.

We had no formal decision process, but we wanted to go fast. Still, there were a few issues. The roadblock on the contracts took a few months to resolve. This may seem a short time, but in a startup, even more, in a *Unicorn's lifetime*, this is an eternity, even more so for a small team.

We had the website contract, the user's agreement, which didn't seem to matter to current visitors. And we had the shareholder agreement which mattered only to me… We had agreed to it earlier on but never finalized nor signed it.

Bak accepted my proposal. Instead of the text made quickly by a lawyer who thought only to protect one party, we had a text-oriented Win-Win that made obligations and responsibilities equivalent.

Here, I would dare a warning to all new entrepreneurs: beware of bad legal texts and ask for fairly balanced text; challenge every unilateral penalty or obligation, and ask why it cannot be equivalent. Be careful of general wording and request precise obligations and responsibilities.

A template is not necessarily a good text, and some are just bad texts perpetuated by the assumption that a template is good! Write a summary of the agreement prior to having an agreement written. The agreement should reflect the business deal, not the other way.

Having solved and signed the shareholder's agreement, I turned my attention to the user's agreement. I was not sure if the user's agreement didn't matter to the visitors: how many were turned back? How many are currently turned back from Facebook because they don't like the legal agreement?

Probably very few, since people don't read contracts: too long, too complicated, too much concentration! I thought about asking data on visitors posting versus those not posting, but what would that say about their perception on the contract?

I guess the main impact was on the partner, me! And maybe other partners who would like to write, but would want to keep their rights. We thought about recruiting social media stars to write in eHappyPedia and I have been thinking about how we could CREATE those stars WITHIN eHappyPedia.

I was thinking back to the time of the creation of my Medical Magazine. Could I use the same recipe: suggesting topics and special angles, giving a little help, motivation and providing social standing and exposure to motivated new writers?

But I could not do this without keeping their author's rights! I could have dropped this fight and hoped that the site's traffic would find some stars organically.

I had tried to think about people I knew that could write and they were, after all, only big bets: friends with zero experience beside dreams, and mostly, totally unknown friends who dreamed of writing but never did and from whom I had never read anything, or celebrities that I wished would accept an interesting proposition. In short, everything was air, thin air.

There was this declining and old lady who had been a famous Canadian author, a specialist of the family affairs, whom I thought would bend for the happiness theme.

There was also a yoga teacher, cute by the way, who always seemed happy, who didn't make it as a model, but in my views, could make it as the image of happiness.

There was the student who wanted to create a new way to build houses: what better opportunity then write some of their ideas in **eHappyPedia** and then move the readers to the full books!

I had some family who could write about how they solved problems or worked through bad times. I would need to help them, but I am good at that: coaching motivating, showing how to do things, drafting the future with them.

But for now, the key writer was Bak, the famous Dr. Bak. He can do a lot, and he writes at an amazing pace, but we were creating a site for the masses, not a personal one.

We needed a machine that would spit dozens and then hundreds of writers, some regulars to sustain the movement, most one-time writers who would leave a small footprint. We needed a few writers to write regularly like Bak.

I got disappointing feedback from the lawyer: essentially proposing no change and asking me to precise my thoughts. Wasn't it clear enough? All the protection was unilateral! It had to be fair, to protect **eHappyPedia**, and to respect the legitimate rights of the authors.

He was asking what legit rights? Well, the right to pull back, but then we needed to make it conditional on reimbursing **eHappyPedia** for the spending that would have been made: say an advertising campaign has been ordered featuring a single sentence and the authors now want to draw back his words because he's now famous!

If **eHappyPedia** created the value, we needed **eHappyPedia** to keep a fair share of the value, but not ALL the value like the lawyer had written.

How do you achieve this? You cannot plan for every circumstance, and you don't even know what could be all the circumstances. I am not an expert in author's right, but surely, JK Rowling didn't give all her rights to Harry Potter follow-ups and movies with her first book.

Problem is we were amateur in this field, and the lawyer was also. With a rate of $700 an hour, conversations with experienced lawyers are quickly becoming very expensive, too expensive!

As in all startups, I ended up writing some legal text. Entrepreneurs always need to be able to read contracts and even write some unless they have a buddy they trust 300% that can do it for them.

Reading means concentrating on every word from the beginning to end, and then, going back to check how definitions are used (important definitions are usually in the contract).

For myself, I always write a cheat sheet of commitments that I find on my way throughout the text, double-checking them by the end of my first reading. Can we respect those obligations?

Dr. JEAN DE SERRES

Above all, I always define what the partnership is for: here it was You write, **eHappyPedia** makes it public. **eHappyPedia** selects a few texts, maybe yours to create advertising.

Whenever we do this, we would add an addendum to the contract, take it or leave it since we don't want to spend legal fees to negotiate or to modify ($700 to negotiate and read the text a couple of times, NO WAY). If you LEAVE, we'll move on to the next text.

That was the solution: a contract for all, and an addendum only for those special selections to give more rights to eHappyPedia in exchange for some benefits to the author: options rather than cash because we had no cash, and options would be linked to the positive effect.

It took 5 months, but I ended up writing the legal system! For now, the energy was going bilateral! Bak was already developing new ideas and hemorraging cash in creating the code and the initial traffic. But we came close to a stop!

Bak had a huge success with the video of his acceptation speech : half a million hit. Within a month time, the sum of all 8 tongues trailer videos of eHappyPedia total more than 2.5 million views. But it faded away as fast as it had arrived. And Bak had to slow down the paid advertisement, buying fewer entries from Facebook and Instagram. Part of it was understandable, even predictable. But it was more than that.

We could have hired statisticians to confirm, but without much money to spend, we could just trust the simple graphs that were laid out in front of me: most people hitting on eHappyPedia were not returning.

It was not a problem with recruitment, but one of retention. "Bak, it is useless to spend more on marketing at this stage!" That was the obvious and inevitable conclusion.

No problem he said, he was running out of money anyway! There was still something to add: content is king! We were betting on the fact that everybody had the desire to write and to share their stories of happiness.

Guess what? The rule of 10 customers for every producer was, once again, verified. Most people wanted to read about somebody else's happiness, not necessarily write their own! We needed more and better content.

How could we do that? Most people writing on our wall were probably soft-spoken and a bit shy and certainly not artists nor influencers. We needed stars, or stars to be: gurus, preachers, salespeople.

We needed action, people wanting to convert others, people wanting to oppose and rebel against… well against something!

"WHAT IF THE KEY WAS NOT HAPPINESS,
BUT THE MOVE TOWARD HAPPINESS?"
Dr. JEAN DE SERRES

Most love movies end up with the wedding scene! They don't tell the history of happiness, but the story of how to get there. We needed more than volunteers: we needed preachers, conversions and passion!

That's good! Now, how do we do that? First, I said, let's copy what worked already. We needed Bak as a star writer: within the two of us, we could take on our shoulders to write and to post to initiate the movement.

Bak is like a guru: he believes, and he can communicate with ease. He is an eternal positive mind, ever optimistic, always energized to try again. Moreover, people listen when he talks!

His image is a great one: the son of an immigrant who succeeds in a new country. Still a visible minority in a minority nation, itself in a minor country beside a giant.

Bak could have rebelled, but he didn't. He is polite, respectful and he made it, not threatening the establishment. He did that while keeping his appeal to the masses.

BAK WILL BE THE GURU, I said!

Dr. Bak will be the public face of **eHappyPedia**, to speak at conferences, at tv shows, why not Oprah? He wrote enough books to create a great story, material to dig from. He was our one and only success!

I believed a smaller public would actually read the books, but they would surely attend the talks, which is better. If we could make Dr. Bak into a success, **eHappyPedia** would also be a success.

Guess what? He was already creating his momentum with his brand, **Dr. Bak**, and he wouldn't need much convincing to sign up! That was the easy part.

As for me, I could write articles, sounded and robust, nothing extravagant, but a positive view on everything, an escape for every fire, a project for every dreamer.

I could dig into my past as a therapist for drug addicts, for victims, for dying patients, to help people survive and find hope. My credibility as a physician and a leader would offer another angle to Bak's. Not in a preacher's way.

He moved quickly from one idea to another, and I moved, well, not as fast. I am a slow writer, nuancing my sentences so that it is 99% exact rather than 90%, exact rather than thrilling. I used to write for medical magazines. I am all about facts and evidence.

But I could commit for a small capsule a day! To fill the space, Bak would create the buzz, I would fill up, propose alternatives, and we would invite guests to comment and to create diversity.

Bak would be doing his buzz with everything he feels like, day after day while I would be building a plan, slowly and steadily. The guests would create the divergent pathways, in opposition, sideways and attract followers.

There would be actions: meetings, conferences, mass-action. Well, 2 or 3 people at a time initially, but with a little chance, we could grow the numbers.

Bak was enthusiastic: he already had 38 books written, a unique story, and he already started his speaking career: we were simply putting the pieces together.

Oh, and we needed a sales staff. A team is signing and gathering the interest of companies as sponsors looking for new ways to catch eyeballs. The content had to be interesting and unique, video or data not linking outside of our site.

Who could do this? Tranie, Bak's wife and partner, vice-president of business development at **Mdex & Co**, ended up with the task. She's an engineer by training and ended up starting businesses with Bak and doing management. She is sweet, analytical, low profile, effective. She was on top of it right away.

She started by meeting all the companies in her building, then with the suppliers and partners of **Mdex & Co**. The offer was simple, we give you free advertising for one year, but we need to approve your content, so it relates to Happiness and fun.

She got negative feedback initially, and we sat down two weeks later to reassess: we decided to go for 2 years of free adds, but with a small setup fee upfront, reimbursable if they ever cancel their participation within the first three months.

We saw a little improvement in our metrics. We got a few articles. Tranie got some sponsoring. Some something…

We also met a bit less frequently. Bak wrote a lot of books and had a few presentations to make. We talked to a few investors who said they would invest. But something was missing!

First, the investors were interested, but not making the next steps. I would have expected specific requests like some more numbers, or meetings with experts in the field, or, of course, a written offer. No, they were only waiting! No action, just wait.

Secondly, we had a few postings, but they were not starting an exponential movement, and they were not generating discussion. A discussion is many postings, but there was none. Traffic without payments to Facebook was disappointing.

Third, sponsoring was not significant as it was mostly individuals saying yes with their small regional budgets, but not the organization's commitments and backup.

My posts were not coming up, and Bak postings were about his books rather than **eHappyPedia**. It was not hitting like the first time. We failed to recruit our theme writers, although we had enough people interested. Something was missing! Everything was volunteer work, and everything was so-so. We needed investment, capital, money!

When you're an experienced entrepreneur, you know that you spend lots of time on some ideas that end up never materializing! Those reading about it in books will often get a bias from the story of success: stories of people who made it lead the reader to believe that those who persist will someday meet with success. Not always. Not on average!

Oh, haven't we already said that ? Well, we will repeat it a number of times: books and movies are wrong about stats!

I look around, and I have a staff member who started two restaurants before quitting to get a regular job as an admin assistant. This one who built a house on his own over 5 years and would never do it again.

Another who bought a 7-Eleven shop, struggled with it for almost 7 years only to sell it. They never rose the bar higher. The 7-Eleven is still on the same corner street! There is no FACEBOOK success there.

Some of these projects take all your free time. It's ok when it's your passion or when you have much fun out of it. But they may damage your family, even your main career, keeping the focus from the real success. In some cases, value is created, but legal fights soon follow.

At that stage, we had Bak and Tranie giving time and injecting some money, a programmer, a media expert, myself, a financial advisor. There were also a few people gathering around whom I was not sure if they were paid: legal, accounting.

In my previous experiences, they were always paid indirectly, and the free service was their way of getting new customers, that's just good public relations.These people had different expectations about being paid someday, one day: a few hoped for thousands, others wanted tens of thousands, most of us sought Millions. For some, it was a chance to get an interesting job. Some already had very high paid jobs.

How were we to organize that mess? Some had contributed key ideas, others had given critical time, others were bouncing bags of ideas. Even secretarial work was important if it was given free!

See, the smallest contribution, if given free, was like a cash injection in the startup company! Which is why these were to be paid in shares, or options.

And since there was a high risk of never getting paid, it made sense to be paid X times the actual input: a RISK FACTOR. Like a lottery ticket. We needed a cap table and a plan to divide the company into its founders!

This should be easy right? But it's not! This is the main enemy of your friendship or partnership. Who is worth what and who contributed what, or even worst, will contribute? The easy cooperative thing does not work most of the time: everyone has an equal share because we're all humans and blablabla…

Maybe it could work if you all have the same assets to start with, pieces of land, pieces of inheritance, but think about teamwork: have you always see everybody doing equal work? How do you compare leadership with support, creativity and a recognized name, accounting with human resources?

And if you survive past that, there is still the part where the investors will decide what the initial team will keep! Bak proposed 25% for his lieutenants like me. Give 15% total to future lieutenants, 10% to upcoming staff, this leaves him with 50% for the idea and first injection of cash. And what do we do with the public injection?

Is it right? Is it wrong? If you think we will beat Facebook someday, you may suggest we don't care because 10% or 50% of Billions is ANYWAY more than what a normal human can spend. But if it ends up being worth 1 Million? Well then…

We had been seeking 20 Millions from investors! Now, we were going to the general public, but for the sake of valuing the company, I suggested that investors would value the company, its team and the ideas at 2 Millions and would take 90% of the company for that investment but the company would be worth 22 Millions then, RIGHT? And 10% would already be worth 2 Millions.

Yeah, Facebook got away with much more, but we are not in Boston or Silicon Valley, and we are not the first Social Media site. But I'm sure Bak would ask for more, much more, so that was good.

It would be a negotiation, and we would have to show that we were worth much more than a simple idea.

I was worried by one thing though: how many people would be shareholders, or significant shareholders and how many key contributions would be required to make it into a real company?

Bak is a great team player, and he has that special touch for gathering people around him. He was the main idea generator. I was the main Administrator and Manager. We had a lead programmer. What else?

Bak would think of many while I would want to keep the lead team to 4 max, maybe 5. So Bak and Tranie, myself, a lead programmer and the next one should be the investor's best friend.

I wanted to leave space for the investor, and I was afraid of 2 things: too many cooks screw the recipe and too many create a **dilution**.

Now, **DILUTION** is the word most entrepreneurs are afraid of, especially those entrepreneurs who need investment. Of course, we are not talking about investors who grow their café with their own money and a bank loan.

We are talking about entrepreneurs who need a lot of cash and who have to turn to cash givers: VC (Venture Capitalists), Angels (Billionaires)! **DILUTION** is what founders are afraid of because obviously, we all want YOU to give your cash at risk and let US make all the money!

Obviously, this is not how things go: CASH GIVERS will invest and charge you the price of the risk, which is the **DILUTION**.

I have met many University Professors who invented a miraculous drug and wanted 200 Million in investment while giving only 20% of the asset!!! You know what? They never got the investment!!!!

127

That is because they teach science and obviously not investment. Because with a 90% risk of failure, the investors will usually take 90% of the company.

Now, this is not a drug and not a pharmaceutical company. We are talking about Social Media, and the risks are as high, but you would not spend the whole 200 Millions right away if you don't get the traffic! The spend would be more progressive, and this gives a chance to mitigate risks.

From that angle, the risk is reduced, greatly reduced.

The risk would be more in the neighbourhood of 2 Millions. On the other hand, the RETURN would be in 2 years, not in 10 years like it might be for a new drug.

When do you get the return is also important: think about it as a pay check: is it the same for you if you get paid only at the end of the year? Of course not!

So how much **DILUTION** does this mean? Pick your guess, that's what we are doing too, an educated guess! Bak asked me how much and whom we should ask. I asked him how much money we needed and how much traffic we would get after a year.

Because we were already searching for the market info and we were getting a good idea of the value of the traffic: how much you're worth with 1 Million visitors, with 1 Million visitors who return to your site, with 1 Million hits?

I had consulted a friend working for a major advertising company, and we had tons of public information from the web, but also from the public report that were mandatory for public companies.

I was crossing the numbers: how much is this company worth, and what are the traffic estimates? I worked out an excel spreadsheet for hours, fixing the template, changing estimates, calculating, and then revisiting some estimates when the results were bad. Everybody does that!

You just corner yourself, assuming unrealistic numbers. With 20 Millions in investment, we would be worth 50 Millions after year one. And if someone would buy that, you would be stuck making your guesses into reality.

Bak didn't need $20M. I did. Because we had different expectations: I added cushions, money for delays, for failure to have successful marketing first time.

I wanted us to be ready for the influx of the public. We could have made a bet with only $1M (that was the minimum we calculated we would need in order to be ready for the **PUBLIC OVERTURE**!) but if the plan sounded that good, why not go for more money and give us a cushion?

TIME TIME TIME, every delay was costing money, adding to the interests, to the costs, decreasing the revenues, adding to the risks! If you don't know that, you need to educate yourself to get your calculations right.

From the management point of view, I needed way more money than Bak, and I assumed fewer returns (this is the profit!) for the investor.

Bak's goal is to get to a win, I guess mine is to get a company running, a serious company. The asset is the company: once you have your own company, you play with the majors, you can borrow, you can fail and restart, you can dream, and you can grow.

**Dr. JEAN DE SERRES**

I made my excel spreadsheet to use 20 Millions in order to get to a 50 Millions valuation. If we could make this into a reality, we would have our investors because they need 2-3X return.

They need to make much more than the 1-2% you get from the bank, since it is guaranteed, more than the 7% you need in a pension fund, because you want growth but not to the point of risking to lose everything, more than the 25% a mobster will require from you before he orders someone to break your legs!

The investors don't get interests nor dividend until they get an EXIT. And the money at the EXIT is the capital plus interest: it should be 200-300%, which is what they call 2X-3X.

It might sound high, but this is because it assumes the risk of bankruptcy in many cases, which is a total loss. With no house as a guarantee, the investor loses ALL the money. The 2-3X will compensate for the loss in the other cases. If our business case didn't show 2-3X returns, we would never get the $20M.

I explained this to Bak, and he was all game for it: they are many obstacles that will damp his enthusiasm! But that investment meant losing control of the company, and in that, he was a wise and crazy optimist: he needed a way to keep control.

Did we have patents? On the coding? On something? On the idea. We tried to brainstorm about it, but we found nothing to patent. That was a big hurt.

Did we have a star founder, a Steve Jobs per se? No, we are "*nobodies*". Even if I have a solid reputation from Quebec's investors, and I am a former CEO of Hema-Quebec and co-founder of 2 biotechs, that was nothing to create a tide!

Our discussions led us to develop the idea that if Bak was to become a star from interviews, books, music, movies, dentistry, ok not dentistry, but everything else, it would help tremendously.

We came with a few ideas:

- To go with the **PUBLIC OVERTURE** (this is the name we gave it to distinguish from public companies that are on the stocks exchange, it is also referring to a piece of music).
- To try to raise $20M **BEFORE** the **PUBLIC OVERTURE**
- To create a buzz: in order to do so, we planned :

  - To leverage the immigrant theme to show an example of successful business and integration, but Bak is no immigrant (Tranie is)! Ok, so we adjusted to an example of success from a visible minority! With a little luck, we could make it to media stardom! On that, he wrote a whole book: **THE CANADIAN SUCCESS**.

131

- To use the narrative of a dentist who became a visionary businessman on social media to make a star out of him! Riskier, who cares about dentists? But he did that too, writing **CHANGING THE WORLD FROM A DENTAL CHAIR.**

Bak proposed to leverage the high suicide rate in dentists to show the importance of **eHappyPedia**. I was not sure this was a good idea because, once more, who cares about dentists?

That is sad, but it doesn't sell as much as the homeless who is suicidal or a famous star with a suspected suicide! Dentists are health providers, and they can CARE, but caring for the mouth doesn't sound as attractive as caring for a patient with cancer!

Dentistry is a hard sell! It might sell when we need them, but it is simply not trendy in our society.

Once again, Bak surprised me with his creativity and dedication. He went on to write **PROFESSION HEALTH**, a book in which I have contributed one chapter.

In that book, he was exploring why health professionals suffered from depression and have suicidal ideas. He even went all the way to launch a research project with the University of Montreal and McGill University, a project that was co-financed between the federal government and his company, **Mdex**. He is a man of means and creativity, I will give him that.

Then, we also explored the idea to use the Happiness theme and start a movement of happy people, better if it was happy-to-be people. I thought the combination of Bak, the dentist, the businessman, the writer, the character was the key of our Buzz.

And of course, Bak wanted to go faster, so we planned to start the **PUBLIC OVERTURE** at the same time we were going after investors. At the same time, Bak was doing his conferences and books. Everything was launching in parallel. Probably stupid but hey, that was the plan!

Let's go in the street
And claim our right to be happy!
Instead of asking for an extra $1
On the minimum wage
Instead of reduced tuition fees
Instead of jobs protection

Because happiness includes everything
Isn't it the real objective after all?
Let's claim our right to be happy!

We thought it was a good idea and we brainstormed about names of would-be stars that could carry the message out loud: Pharrell Williams because of his song, Happy, Bell Canada for their fight against depression, Amelie Poulain (the movie that makes you happy!), Snoopy (but he would not be available), to name a few.

That was good, but we needed to be practical and get names that could really be partners in our project.

Another idea was to use a perfect stranger, a little girl with a big smile who would start giving free smiles and messages of hope downtown, first to randomly picked people, then adding preselected followers (arranged in advance with our friends) and then to a journalist (random appearance of course), and a few good Facebook relays.

This could work! A bit like Gandhi's passive resistance movement or Mao's Long Walk. Weren't these big marketing campaigns? To use our **eHappyPedia** network to recruit initial followers, to create a gathering, to have a walk every Sunday morning to claim happiness, to live happiness, to talk about it. What an idea!

Sunday morning is perfect as it can help churches who want their followers back to the mass. It can help families to gather for the Sunday brunch, it's a quiet media day, making it easier to have the spotlight, and no sport event competing in the morning either! It sounds more and more as a great idea!

Those were all ideas without any boundaries nor limitation. We decided that there were two good options for our goal of creating existing value for the brand of **eHappyPedia**: Sunday morning **eHappy** gathering or to have Bak as a writer and speaker.

Finally, we decided on the second option. If it worked well, we could have a name for us, with credibility and value, when we would meet with investors.

We would ask them 20 Million in investment for 50% of the company. We would go public with our plan and progress, and the **PUBLIC OVERTURE** (I also thought we should write a piece of music on that theme!) would compete with the VC fundraising.

Wow, a valuation of 40 Millions (if they buy half for 20 Millions, the whole is worth 40 Millions right ?) for **eHappyPedia**! We drifted for a few moments and started thinking about fantasies: nice offices in a high rise downtown, business class visits to affiliates worldwide, children growing up to succeed us in the family business…

We would soon need a fiscal structure, how is this called, an optimal fiscal structure, with an affiliate in Barbados or Cayman and another in Island. Wasn't Ireland the place to go for famous authors in order to protect royalties that would be generated by the postings?

That was only a plan, and some well-known thinkers have said: Execution is everything!

We needed execution!

This is **eHappyPedia, THE RISE OF THE UNICORN.** Are you ready for a better tomorrow?

HAPPINESS IS A
STATE OF MIND
THAT EMPOWERS
OUR BELIEFS

HAPPINESS IS THE FIRST STEP TO
CONFIDENCE
OR VICE VERSA
THAT'S THE COOL PART WITH
HAPPINESS

IT'S NOT ABOUT WORDS OR
ORDER
TRUE HAPPINESS IS
A FEELING
DEMANDING TO BE
SHARED

# CHAPTER 8

## "ON THE WAY TO FIND MOMENTUM"

by Dr. BAK NGUYEN

**Momentum**, that's my secret power, well, not that secret anymore... Momentum is the only way I know how to move forward and to find success. So how can I find or build momentum for **eHappyPedia**?

Jean was pretty clever to use my momentum as a writer to "*reanimate*" **eHappyPedia**. It took me a few chapters, but it worked.

I was working on my own books and Jean wanted to reanimate **eHappyPedia**. Now, we were creating a start-up-book. I won't lie, that book would prove to be one of the hardest I had to write since my emotional and mathematical intelligence did not align from the beginning.

"INSPIRATION IS WHEN YOUR INTELLIGENCES ALIGNED."
Dr. BAK NGUYEN

So it was time for me to bet once again, on myself. I use the word bet, but really, the right two words would be: **LEVERAGE** & **CONFIDENCE**.

"TO BET IS TO LEVERAGE AND TO HAVE CONFIDENCE... IN ONESELF. OTHERWISE, IT IS A SIMPLE GAMBLE... AND I DON'T GAMBLE."
Dr. BAK NGUYEN

But before I would commit to **eHappyPedia** as a book-start-up, I wanted to start another project. I told you that my next move, as for the books, was to make LIVE videos to leverage on what **Mdex** and **Dr. Bak**'s brands were exploring at this stage.

I proposed it both in writing and through a phone conversation to Jean. I wasn't sure of the outcome of that conversation...

If it wasn't for the time constraint, he would be all in! I was speechless! Trust me, that does not happen too often. Jean was embracing the opportunity and the day, even more than I was.

From his last chapter, Execution is everything, I could see that he slept on the idea and went all-in with the idea of broadcasting live the entrepreneurial journey of eHappyPedia.

His enthusiasm writing as he kept sending me his chapters day after day reanimated the beating heart of eHappyPedia that I had put on the back burner.

In one of his chapter, he mentioned that I am a marketing mind. Ok, I'll take it! Let's leverage on that. Over the years, I refined my ways to communicate: movies, website, adds, texts, books, videos, conferences...

If I take a closer look, there are two main threads coming back again and again: a message and a narrative structure. Can a message and a narrative structure put eHappyPedia back on track? This is worth it!

Why not? I am now eager to write my next chapter, still not sure of what it will be about though. To write the future, this time, I will follow his lead, to leverage on myself, my skill set as a communicator.

The core message, at least of this start-up-book, would be an adventure trying to use friendship and respect, to keep a great and noble idea alive, despite the odds.

He would be telling his side of the story as he is walking the words as he put them on paper. I would do the same. He would explain, analyze, and plan. I would feel, drive and empower.

Happiness is a great subject of uttermost importance. But it is so vast and has so many faces. The rebirth of **eHappyPedia** would be a story of friendship and of seizing the day with what we have, bet and leveraged with what is available now, on the table.

That's for the beautiful words and positive thinking! But there was another obstacle. **eHappyPedia** had been launched in the wake of **EmotiveNow**, but the team was no longer. It had been dismissed.

How do you make a platform now that the engineering team has long been discharged? **eHappyPedia** has now a bare minimum support team of consultants, Jean and myself.

One morning, I woke up at 5 AM to write. I took my shower and realized that I also had to make a LIVE video since I missed the day before. You see, I had promised to make one LIVE a day for the next month.

Between the writing, the correction, the editing of the other books so they could finally be published on iTunes and Amazon, not to forget my daily as CEO and dentist, I was starting to run out of time… and energy.

Those last days, it was either to write or to do a LIVE video. It's not a matter of time, but of brainpower, of creative juice. But a little earlier that week, something magical happened.

First, I have to put you in context. We are today April 12th. By April 24th, I will be giving my first Dr. Bak's event as the main anchor in front of 600-700 people.

Trust me, the number is huge for a first timer. Sure I've given speaking events in the past, but I was just a speaker, not the only anchor and not the one having to fill up the seats.

The LYS of diversity, The John Molson School of Business, Concordia University, the Olympic Stadium, the Influence United, the LinkedIn & Town Hall award, those were all organized by experts. I just had to show up and to empower the crowd.

This time, my team and I have to fill up the seats. And 700 people, that would be the biggest crowd ever assembled by Dr. Bak, for Dr. Bak. I am not bragging, if anything, I am freaking out at the idea that the event will not be completely sold out.

So because of that, my team succeeded to have me promise to do one LIVE video a day. I did that for about a week, and I will for a month, maybe not a LIVE a day, but an average of one a day. Flexibility, that's how I make my numbers and my promises work.

By the time I was at my 6th LIVE, an old friend and podcaster, HUGO PRINCE, came by at my office to congratulate me. He joined in the LIVE with my Director of Event, Jonas Diop, the head of my event of the 24th.

As we had fun talking on camera, Hugo was amazed of how I made my LIVE video worked, with minimum gears and support and still, with a Dr. Bak's touch, straight out of Hollywood.

I showed him everything. Hugo has been a podcaster for years now, he appreciated the sharing. By the end of the LIVE video, he asked me why don't I go audio with PODCAST?

I would have told him how over my head I am deep in right now, but I held back my words, and I listened.

He told me about a way to extract the audio from my LIVE sessions to publish them as PODCASTS, internet radio. He even showed me all the tools and platforms he was using.

I welcomed his generosity, and I smiled. To be honest, I appreciated him sharing, but I didn't think that I could take on anything else. The next day, I woke up at 5 AM, ready to write. After the shower, I opened my computer and I saw the sites Hugo left open on my laptop.

I gave it a try. That morning, I didn't write anything…

By 7 AM, I had a PODCAST setup and ready to be published. I put five of my LIVE into PODCAST episodes and within the next days, I received confirmation of my presence on Apple Podcast, Google Podcast, Spotify Podcast and all the other major platforms that I still have a hard time remembering their names.

Oh, and I must give credit to the minds behind the LIVE. Movie Director Justin Morganstein and Strategist Jonas Diop both pushed me to embrace that medium for months now.

Justin helped me with the initial setup and Jonas with the anchoring preparation. They all brought their best to the table. I have a great team I can reach for, I just need to put eHappyPedia in the EYE of my attention.

So here is the dare I will take today. I will surf the rebirth of **eHappyPedia** throughout LIVE videos, Podcasts, and this book. It will be about creating a community and empowering a strong message first, and we will rebuild the platform later.

Well, people can always use our pilot online at **www.ehappypedia.com**. It is functional and powerful when you know how to use it and leverage from it.

Far from perfect and will need much love, capital and attention to grow into the conscience of our generation,  but let's give it a voice through mine, Jean and my friends!

Today was the first episode of **MILLION DOLLAR MINDSET**, my podcast, talking about **eHappyPedia**, the book, and the endeavor. Many more will follow this idea of sharing and spreading happiness! And wish me luck for the 24th!

This is **eHappyPedia**, **THE RISE OF THE UNICORN.** Are you ready for a better tomorrow?

HAPPINESS IS A
STATE OF MIND
THAT EMPOWERS
OUR BELIEFS

HAPPINESS IS THE FIRST STEP TO
CONFIDENCE
OR VICE VERSA
THAT'S THE COOL PART WITH
HAPPINESS

IT'S NOT ABOUT WORDS OR
ORDER
TRUE HAPPINESS IS
A FEELING
DEMANDING TO BE
SHARED

# CHAPTER 9
## "THUS MY STAND"
by Dr. JEAN DE SERRES

It is said that great projects require two people, a **DREAMER** and an **EXECUTIVE**. In Hollywood, they called them director and producer, artist and businessman.

It's a simplistic summary. The **DREAMER** need long term energy, a bit like marathon runners. Many of us can dream for an hour or two, and then get sucked back to our daily... to finally forget everything about our dreams.

The real **Entrepreneur Dreamer** needs to remember and to believe in his dreams after the awakening! And to be able to dream the same dream over and over again.

Then, he will need to transfer that energy to his team, for days, weeks, months and years. So maybe he should be called a **MOTIVATIONAL DREAMER**!

But to materialize, even the best dreams requires **EXECUTION.** What is the next small step put into action? And the next one, and the one after that? One step at a time, like the *PETIT POUCET* creating a path between now and his dream: With thousands of little rocks, one rock at a time!

These ideas and their application were great concepts, but everything requires security, reliability and robustness. In other words, money and infrastructure that we didn't have.

## SLOWING DOWN

Suddenly, I felt like slowing down. Because Bak is living at such a frenzy pace! Is it hyperactivity, attention deficit disorder, ambition, drugs, or else? It is **Happiness**, his *joie de vivre*.

I started wondering if we needed to slow down to better feel the project, the happiness.

## SLOWING DOWN
### by JEAN DE SERRES

Relaxing,
Listening without talking,
Observing without moving,

Thinking without analyzing,
Just feeling the moment,
Feeling *eHappy*!

Feeling it like a song
Slowly growing into your mind,
Gently rocking your day,

No time, no schedule, no appointment,
No need, just slowing down.
Feeling *eHappy*!

The more I was getting into it, the more I felt we needed it. Can you feel your company, your achievement, your creation? Can you feel the satisfaction of what you've done?

I guess it's important, for the commitment, for the creativity, for the energy.

Wow, just thinking about getting Bak to slow down and to watch peacefully his organization grow, the web lighting up, just watching it becoming, like watching a movie, all in passivity, in receptive-mode, in feed mode, that would be a challenge by itself! Is that even possible ???

When you're in that state, you see memories coming back, ideas forgotten, ideas transformed. Not ideas like actions, rather ideas like a movie passing on the screen: wow, this one is good, and this one, maybe not that much…

"REPLENISH YOURSELF TAKING THE TIME TO SEE IDEAS PASSING AS A MOVIE AND WATCH IT GROW ON ONE. THAT'S A KEY TO CREATIVITY"

Dr. JEAN DE SERRES

That's a great feeling
Almost like a drug
Feeling of the fun
Hope talking

Dreaming
Setting up
Arguing
Slowing down...

149

That was the thing to do. Just because we needed to do things differently. I started this book boldly saying how Bak and I were different and how we are using that difference to create.

Not doing something for one chapter in the existence of eHappyPedia is the perfect antithesis, like the immaculate White Album, was the answer to the overcrowded Sergeant Pepper. Just like a good night sleep between two crazy days. That is my take and my stand!

I was thinking about how to prolong that peace and calm: meditation, music, a walk in the park. How can we transpose this moment into a cornerstone in the eHappyPedia's construction process?

I am convinced that we needed to act as observers: see the guy watching the birds, while we are watching him! But I couldn't find a purpose for this *slowness*. How could we use that to grow faster?

Obviously, I needed to avoid being too analytical! Watch out, don't stay away, stay focused on being non-focused, SLOW and meditative. When you compete, don't be predictable! If your enemy expects you to be somewhere, be somewhere else.

When you trust the GPS, Facebook and Google will know exactly what you are going to do this morning, where and when you will be driving to work, to grocery, to the coffee shop, this is when you need to steer away and do the unexpected.

I felt we had to slow down, just because we were going fast, just because we had to be creative and unexpected! The art of war…

Everyone starting a new social network is basically doing the same thing: programming a platform, branding with a flashy name, inventing a new feature even minor, that will distinguish you from others.

Dr. JEAN DE SERRES

Since there are thousands of startups all wishful that they are the next Facebook, if thousands launch at the same time, I know for sure that they are to going to make it. The world is one big league with one champion. ONE.

So, we could not follow the business plan book we had written. It's unfortunate because I felt it was a great book, clear, and true. But Bak was going too fast into new projects. Our project had changed already.

I had two options, trying to get him to stop his mind from flowing into new directions, new fields, and focus, focus, focus. Or lose him! Actually, by listening to him and to his books projects, and recently to his video and podcast projects, I found a third option: to integrate all of it. His ideas, making the project a Dr. Bak's project. And the start-up-book project was created.

It was then easy to say yes to his video project, podcasts, conferences: all were easily integrated into the start-up book. We had to write backwards all of the roads quickly travelled so far, and even before I was done with my parts, as usual, Bak was already into the present, that it is, into future directions, new projects.

He was speaking present tense when I was still describing the past leading to this new present. And I could feel the disconnection. The initial reaction is always: that's bad!

But, then, trying to integrate and create a new from this duo of differences, I thought, that is exactly what the young businessperson need to learn: manage different people, and to create value out of obstacles.

We had lived a quick but short-lived success. I was not done with the description of the past story of our **eHappyPedia** project, now revamped as a book-start-up (or start-up-book!). We had no real programming team. We had not executed our fundraising plan either. But we had a better concept!

And **eHappyPedia** still made sense. The problem was, as the business schools will teach anyone, **EXECUTION**. But the **PUBLIC OVERTURE** plan or start-up-book project were the solutions integrating Bak's personality and behaviors as strengths and leverage into our business plan.

The concept was to create the company in the public eye through the writing (also public) of a book-video-story. This would also serve as our key fundraising strategy.

Crazy concept. And in a few days, we had written the missing part of the book (chapters precedent) in expectation of our public opening. And now, right before this public opening, I needed to take a deep breath!

Actually, it is the best stimulant and a good simulation too! Writing this book got **eHappyPedia** back in Bak's attention. It reminds us of all the things we need to keep in mind: finance, legal, human resource, friendship, enemies, bureaucrats, the acts of God, the psychology of the market, of why customer A will pay a higher price then customer B. The book explains everything.

I felt like doing the unexpected, like slowing down against all the odds. Not because I was tired, not out of depression, not by distraction. I slowed down out of instinct. It was meditation.

Running like Forest Gump
Skiing in the blizzard
Making peace with
Our Canadian Winters.

Visiting friends,
Eating and talking about everything
Without doing anything
Without any plan...

This is my take and my view, the way I see eHappyPedia, how it feels and its future. That's my take of happiness.


## The tipping point


In practice, our first action out of the new PUBLIC OVERTURE plan was to adjust the price for sponsors, based on our success forecast. The old Colonel Parker's trick is: charge double with a 50% discount, it will sell more than a regular low price! It worked! We got 12 sponsors.

Next, we used our renewed motivation to deliver. By that time, I had 14 capsules online and Bak, two more books written and a promising conference and we were posting links on **eHappyPedia**.

Now our programmers had something to play with. With the vibe of renewal, we got the artists in and have a visual lift done to **eHappyPedia**. It's got some red, some pink, bits of blue and yellow. Exciting maybe for there was no relaxing green or not much blue. But we wanted attention, not sleepy readers! The site looked better, refreshed.

This is **eHappyPedia, THE RISE OF THE UNICORN.** Are you ready for a better tomorrow?

HAPPINESS IS A
STATE OF MIND
THAT EMPOWERS
OUR BELIEFS

HAPPINESS IS THE FIRST STEP TO
CONFIDENCE
OR VICE VERSA
THAT'S THE COOL PART WITH
HAPPINESS

IT'S NOT ABOUT WORDS OR
ORDER
TRUE HAPPINESS IS
A FEELING
DEMANDING TO BE
SHARED

# CHAPTER 10
## "SHARING IS THE WAY TO GROW"

by Dr. BAK NGUYEN

It had been several days since I wrote anything. I wasn't slowing down but I was exhausted and empty. Between the LIVES, the preparation of the events and the stress of filling up those 700 seats…

It did not felt that great to have an interruption of inspiration. What was once a momentum allowing me to surf the storms and the days, now felt like a burden on my shoulders.

"THE DAY IT IS EASIER TO GO ON THAN TO STOP,
THAT DAY YOU'VE REACHED MOMENTUM."

Dr. BAK NGUYEN

For my defence, I wasn't sitting on my hands. April 24th was taking most of my juice and creativity. It would be the first time that people came to see Dr. Bak. I had done many speaking events before, but I was participating, not creating one. This time, it was a Dr. Bak's event.

700 people, that's a lot of people, a lot! When I booked the room, I knew it would be a challenge. I wanted to make a statement, to make sure that Dr. Bak would have a great start in the world of motivational speaking. And I set the bar pretty high!

It started great, 100 tickets were gone within the first 48 hours. Then, another 100 within the following week. And then, it slowed down. I was worried, I had to step up my game.

I was doing LIVES podcast in Jonas Diop' show, **Duc, DEVIENS EMPEREUR.** But the tickets were still not flying off of the shelf. We were stuck in the 200s. Then, something happened.

Jean was very committed to write **eHappyPedia** and had started writing a retrospective, hoping to catch up with the present soon.

Knowing that I have to live up to each of the words I write, I looked for ways to merge my paths, making my entrance in the speaking world a step for **eHappyPedia**.

Last Sunday, I went on air to talk openly about **eHappyPedia** and shared the idea with my new found audience. The reception was timid. But with so many LIVE SESSIONS piling up, it wasn't easy to single one out.

Still in the hundreds, both my audiences and the tickets sold, it felt like I had reached a wall.

Then, a magical thing happened, just because I kept my posts and my enthusiasm. People started to reach out. More and more friends showed up at my office to join in my LIVE SESSIONS. They wanted to join the vibe.

Some brought their friends; all were dying to meet with the *famous Dr. Bak*. Seriously, I had no clue what was going on, I was simply going with the flow and keeping my eyes on the ball: filling up those 700 seats.

William, my son, happily took his place as a regular contributor. In his mind, this was our show... Jonas, Justin were regulars too. I came to meet with a SUPERSTAR FOOTBALL PLAYER of the CFL, CANADIAN FOOTBALL LEAGUE, Christophe Mulumba.

Christophe went on to share about business in one of my LIVE SESSION and tagged me as his mentor the following days in the social media.

TV Host, Malik Shaheed showed up at one of my LIVE SESSION and set the house on fire, ON-AIR! Those are the big guns. I also met with many entrepreneurs just enchanted that someone like me was sharing with them. I had fans, and it was my first time meeting with them!

For years, I used to struggle, to walk against the winds and the odds, to deal with jealousy, doubts and uncertainty. To be welcomed by fans, that was surely something new, to me!

I used all that love and energy to fuel my LIVE SESSIONS, sharing more and more about SUCCESS and feeling HAPPY to do so. On eHappyPedia, we had a whole magazine dedicated to SUCCESS, eHappyPedia SUCCESS. This was my contribution.

I SURFED THE WAVE AND MASTERED MY SKILLS
THEN, THE WAVE BECAME BIGGER, AND I WAS READY

Dr. BAK NGUYEN

You would think that this would be the core of this chapter. You thought wrong. Happiness attracts happiness!

In all my books, I said that SHARING IS THE WAY TO GROW. I will soon have another proof of that wisdom! First, it was PODCASTER Hugo Prince who shared his art and craft, allowing me to make PODCAST out of my LIVE SESSIONS.

Then, the public following Jonas and Christophe started following me. More and more people were watching my SHOW and listening to my PODCAST. More and more people were joining in the vibe.

If I needed a reminder, William was asking every day when he would be making his next LIVE SESSION! The **Momentum** outgrew me, with all my skills and my training. It was now time for me to let go and to embrace the wave of positivity!

You see, I had a pretty good excuse to explain the slowing down of my writings. Especially since I had to provoke things in my daily life to have something worthwhile to write about! All of that while still being real and authentic, loyal to my words and to my core.

So what's next? The vibe was there, the **Momentum** is palpable, not only by me but also the friends, fans and followers.

How many startups can brag about having a public and a great vibe to welcome their birth or rebirth? I thought this was too great to miss. Jean was right from the beginning, I just needed to bring back eHappyPedia at the center of my attention.

The next few days were crucial to me. Easter's weekend was coming, and with that, I had a long weekend to prepare for my rebirth. So it should be eHappyPedia's too.

Jean told me not to talk about the **PUBLIC OVERTURE** concept yet. Well, it doesn't come naturally, spontaneously. But the pendulum was moving in the right direction, and that was a start.

Then, I took the decision. My Podcast, LIVE SESSIONS, and the upcoming event would be co-sponsored by **Mdex** and eHappyPedia.

I was the chairman of both companies and, this time, I would not compromise my decision not to ask for permission. As Dr. Bak, I would take **Momentum** to push both eHappyPedia and **Mdex** to the main public, to the love of our audience, my audience!

The first thing to do was to redesign all the communications to include the logo of eHappyPedia. On screen, it would have to appear as the main player.

How about doing it like the DISNEY - PIXAR's association? But this time, it would not be the result of the fight between two titans, Steve Jobs, and Michael Eisenberg. It was a decision of conviction and courage. Both **Mdex** and eHappyPedia promise to change the world for the better.

**Mdex** was at a stage of maturity, and the concept was taking roots and gaining interest and steam. eHappyPedia had the power of *contagious sympathy* and versatility. Versatility…

To make it work, I would have to be the bigger man. I would need to rise as **Dr. Bak**. Not just the *cosmic dentist* and the visionary CEO, but as a mark of *audacity* and of *consistency* all at once.

I was already out there writing books and sharing my thoughts. The first time I went public to take over a goal was when I started posting every day my swimming laps. 20 laps day, for a whole summer. Cold or warm, sunny or rainy, I was posting my laps.

Those laps, later on, were replaced by chapters. Day one and two, and four and ten, my posts were coming in. Chapter by chapter, I became an author. Book after book, I wrote my story and marked history as a side effect. I worked all my life to achieve this **Momentum**. Why not take this next bet?

"FIND THE WAY TO SYNERGY, NOT JEALOUSY."
Dr. BAK NGUYEN

I would have to be stronger, wiser, bolder since my attention would be divided. I'm sorry, should have said multiplied (I am still adjusting to my new role). But to make it, I still had an ace in my sleeve, a power of my own, my ability to grow **Momentums**.

This is my time
My time to share
My time to be
My time to give back

And what do I have to give back?
My energy and my heart.

This is **eHappyPedia, THE RISE OF THE UNICORN.** Are you ready for a better tomorrow? I Am!

HAPPINESS IS A
STATE OF MIND
THAT EMPOWERS
OUR BELIEFS

HAPPINESS IS THE FIRST STEP TO
CONFIDENCE
OR VICE VERSA
THAT'S THE COOL PART WITH
HAPPINESS

IT'S NOT ABOUT WORDS OR
ORDER
TRUE HAPPINESS IS
A FEELING
DEMANDING TO BE
SHARED

# CHAPTER 11

## "POPULATING THE IDEA"

by Dr. JEAN DE SERRES

The first article we posted under this new plan was about *Hallmark-like movies*. Do you know them? Have you seen any of them?

These are very easy going, low-cost movies defined as anti-Marvel or anti-Hollywood in the sense that they are about social situations with a systematic happy ending and no really dangerous character or real threat destroying the world. I believe they started as Hallmark spin-off but were soon copied by many.

If these movies never make it to the Oscars or on the top of the box-office, they are still appealing enough for quite a sizeable portion of the population.

Those movies are never discussed by the critics, totally forgotten by the media in general, but they are surviving very well. This is a niche, a niche of people in *need of happiness*.

If you like a *Hallmark-like movies* once in a while, if you have fun watching an old Elvis movie, as bad as they are rated, you are proof that they are still relevant 60 years later!

There is now a place where you can talk about them, those cheesy feeling good movies! What's your favorite *Hallmark-like movie*? Call your friends and organize an evening of 3 *Hallmark-like movies* marathon with lots of popcorn, home variants with curry, truffles and chocolate!

Actually, why not host a watching party on the eHappyPedia network? We would need a legal agreement with the producers of that movie and I will have to talk to Bak to know if it is possible.

**Dr. JEAN DE SERRES**

We had this idea of getting *Hallmark or a similar company* to post a link to us and from us to them. We asked a University professor to compare how many clichés you could find in a *Hallmark-like movie* but we also asked them to do the same with a Marvel movie !

A great surprise to all of us: the Marvel won with a good margin for the highest number of clichés. Many said non-clichés are actually strong clichés, starting with villains that are just that, villains and all powerful! We got a spot for Bak on a radio station to discuss the results.

**Dr. JEAN DE SERRES**

It was only after a few days that we thought about a link with the TV website which hosted these movies. How about having people commenting and posting their feedbacks on **eHappyPedia**!

I wrote the next day about the difficulty of saying out loud how hard it is to simply express that those movies were making us feel better!

To stimulate answers, well, we poked a few people, first in our respective offices. Some feedbacks were only verbal, but we cheated a bit and wrote them as genuine direct feedbacks. We didn't change the wording, we just put them in writing.

The following day, a strange article appeared on the site: about the lack of happiness in the mandatory books from the minister of education program in high school: 4 out of 5 included a suicide in their story! How depressing! And right on with my personal experience (my kids actually).

I still believe this article was anonymous because someone took the concept from me. But I don't own it, like most of our ideas, or observations. That was an observation, only that.

I suggested the fight against suicide should start by removing the halo around it and by highlighting happy ending stories. We made it into a letter for the most important newspapers. Bak got an appointment on the spot to give an interview about it.

He was also organizing meetings about happiness with a few friends, therapists and gurus. We included the famous concept of **eHappyMeditation** for the first time.

Write a happy thing, first thing in the morning, on a piece of paper, on your phone or iPad. Think about it at your morning break, at lunch, at the afternoon break, and dinner, at least a glimpse of it each time. Above all, before going to sleep, think that you will dream about it that night. That's the **eHappyMeditation** with a call to action.

Day after day, you build your **eHappiness** through meditation. Well, the concept of meditation existed before, as well as the concept of thinking about happy things as I had thought about my depressed patients.

But it was never packaged with a great brand name, an easy formula, and a supportive web site. That's our take! We suggested to post the morning happy thought on eHappyPedia: it could be scheduled as a reminder in one click, and it would make it more memorable.

We connected with an App a One Hundred Days Fitness Challenge for special groups and companies. Since it included a recommendation to have a positive thought every day and a meditation-like activity daily, it was a good fit with eHappyPedia. Actually, we found many more similar programs and got some to link back to us.

Well, people should use eHappyPedia as a vision board, a place to hang the wishful thoughts to the universe and to themselves.

CONNECTION BOARD: with some budget, I am looking to push our engineers to have automated reminders and ways to connect together people with similar thoughts and goals.

I just mentioned the idea and Bak is already having a solution for connecting people. That's is something I appreciate from in my partnership: efficiency!

We already recruited 13 of the targeted 19 writers for our 19 magazines concepts. Unfortunately, this idea did not grow as expected. Simply put, we had to press some friends to accept the position and they were writing a few posts, without much substance, and mostly, without attracting feedback.

Dr. Bak was still the main driver with all his books and friends. But, as a manager, I didn't want a single author as a steam machine but rather a 20 power horses engine.

Now, the 14th author will be the couple Jean and Bak and the posts, the chapters of this book on our journey riding **eHappyPedia**. It was still too early to judge how this would work. Remember, the number was our ticket to success.

With the progress of artificial intelligence, I can already see people sharing the same issue at the same time connecting with each other and serving as support group! The possibilities are within reach. The needs are, well just open your eyes, all around you!

As a physician, I am pretty convinced that **eHappyPedia** might have a chance to help the health system and the high rate of depression and isolation in our societies. Hey, maybe we could have some help from the government on that matter? Why not?

"BELIEVE WHAT YOU MUST, BUT BELIEVE IN SOMETHING."
Dr. JEAN DE SERRES

We decided to task someone to look for grants at different levels: federal, provincial, municipal, charity, foundations, even research-sponsoring organizations.

We also decided to give a new officer the responsibility to find the extra magazine's leaders we needed.

We were going short on money though! And that was worrisome. At some point, we would have to quit. But we found new ways to avoid paying for anything, and getting new volunteers and future partners (who didn't have yet a clear agreement other than the verbal promise).

We used a lot of free services, switching providers in some cases just to get the free 3 months or free 1 year (better!).

Were all these decisions easy to make? No! Since we came up with hundreds of ideas. Some were crazy and easy to write off, I always like to start with the easy steps and obvious ones first.

Some were interesting but required serious investment: we filed them as nice to have, in the SHOULD column. Some were easy and needed time: we simply asked who would have the time? Bak always has time, and I always have none, which means you cannot trust those answers!

"TOO MANY YES MEANS DELAYS AND TOO MANY NO MEANS AFTERTHOUGHTS."
Dr. JEAN DE SERRES

Our discussion was never heated: probably because we don't take ourselves too seriously. No one wants to die for his idea, no one wants to die with a great idea in mind either!

We were the two of us, sometimes with friends and partners. Coffee, juice, rarely a drink.

And finally, we started posting the story behind this venture, behind this company. That was chapter 1. Bak finally found a way to talk about the concept of **PUBLIC OVERTURE** in his talks and podcasts.

It was not so easy: not telling the whole story as this was not the topic, mentioning enough to tease, acknowledging the concept is not so obvious, and not easy to be translated into 3 sentences or 2 words.

We created a few posts referring to the chapter. We got a second chapter out. Then we hit on the need to have a contract for ourselves! If we believe in success, let's have a contract.

It was a simple one, very simple, just saying we shared the book and all its relatives or formats 50-50, every change to be agreed by both names. That's all.

But what about the rights to the sequel? Indeed, this is a tad arrogant since I guessed our chances of success were 1 in 100! It had to be 50-50 but did we grant each other a veto right. After all, this was what Roger Water asked for when he left his ex-bandmates to go on with the name Pink Floyd!

If there is veto right, then each can do whatever they want with the product sequels, so we decided for a veto right on sequels. And what about presentations about the book?

We decided this one had to be trusted on friendship, and there would be no veto. And successions? If I die tomorrow, do I transfer a veto right to a spouse? We said yes. Ouff, not so simple, but ok.

We had already chapter 2 posted. This is no wishful thinking, this is the cure to the world's disease of drama and depression.

As a physician, this is my take, this is my stand.

This is eHappyPedia, THE RISE OF THE UNICORN.

HAPPINESS IS A
STATE OF MIND
THAT EMPOWERS
OUR BELIEFS

HAPPINESS IS THE FIRST STEP TO
CONFIDENCE
OR VICE VERSA
THAT'S THE COOL PART WITH
HAPPINESS

IT'S NOT ABOUT WORDS OR
ORDER
TRUE HAPPINESS IS
A FEELING
DEMANDING TO BE
SHARED

# CHAPTER 12
## "THE POWER OF PERCEPTION"

by Dr. BAK NGUYEN

You started reading this book wishing to learn how to build a bluechip company rising fast, a unicorn. Dr. De Serres initiated this project because he wanted to see actions and to materialize a vision. I started the writing out of respect to my mentor.

As you read through the previous chapters, this is also a journey very personal to each of us. We thought of removing many personal passages to have a smoother reading and a better experience throughout the general flow of the narrative. Well, we both resisted to look good and to press DELETE.

Happiness is a personal journey that each of us must embrace when ready. How can you empower the walk to happiness if you suppress the thought process leading to the revelation?

Jean wrote in a previous chapter that happiness is about the journey, not the destination. So this is our journey, and we are sharing it with you, unfiltered, may be edited and polished, but as raw as possible, closer, not to the truth, but to what we feel deeply.

From Jean's slowing down and meditation to my hesitation and reluctance at the beginning, you read the words, and you felt the emotions. You are sharing what it is like to be in our shoes, our brains and our hearts. Actually, in our company.

Whatever words Jean and I are using, the conclusion is the same: we are now in motion, and from actions, we can build **Momentum**.

That I know. Going from Jean's chapter to mine, we can all feel the dichotomy and the differences between our mindsets. Jean said it at the beginning of this endeavor: we are fundamentally two different people.

Going through Jean's, you had a better understanding of how a startup is weighted, how it is valued, and how it might pick up from the ground. Jean has the knowledge and the connections to build a real company, a sustainable company.

Dr. JEAN DE SERRES

On the other hand, you've followed me through my days, my challenges and my emotions. It was the first time that I shared in-depth my emotional process going through the birth of a company, or to be precise, the decision making process.

As Jean was building on the logic and the numbers, I was all about the feelings and the drive... and something about the doubt before the resolution. This is also a logical process, but mine is deeply rooted in my emotional intelligence.

Because this is what I've learned launching businesses and endeavors, the words are unique and different for each project. The numbers will then tell you another story, one of the promised lands. But, at the end of the day, it is the control and the discipline of the leaders who will make or break a company.

Take any builder's story, take away the words, strip away the numbers, and surprise! You will find the same spine to the story, just like a script from Hollywood. The emotional story is often the same!

Spark · Doubts · Resolutions · Actions · Tests · Darkness · Decision

Don't laugh, it is the exact same way that we are making legends and movie scripts. Here is the same path in emotional mapping:

**Empowerment - Fear - Confidence - Passion - Exhaustion - Discouragement - Courage/Pride**

And what is **Momentum**? Leverage from emotions, no? Or in emotional mapping: **DOUBTS** and **GREET**. That's why it was so hard to calculate everything and why logic cannot always be applied. You can have the perfect plan, but when it boils down to pull the trigger, can you do it, at the required moment? I could.

I could in my own disciplined way, work for long hours on an idea, focus all my energies on the spot while Jean was thinking about it, turning it upside down and analyzing it. He is the marathon runner, disciplined in a different way. His long rumination could spoil the Momentum. And he probably felt that I took some turns without looking at my death angle. We made a good pair. And we executed!

On that, we both agree, Jean and I. Execution is everything! Let's add that timing is the essence of success. **EXECUTION** and **TIMING**. To execute, one needs a plan and the intelligence to keep his focus and discipline. Ok, Jean said that timing was out of our hands unless we had prepared for this moment. But I was up to sense the right time, the right opportunity. And those increasing numbers of hits were making me right.

Dr. BAK NGUYEN

We had gone through the complete dilemma of each entrepreneur before this big break, before any break. The emotions and mapping are the same in all the stories.

This is eHappyPedia, **THE RISE OF THE UNICORN.** Are you ready for a better tomorrow? I Am!

HAPPINESS IS A
STATE OF MIND
THAT EMPOWERS
OUR BELIEFS

HAPPINESS IS THE FIRST STEP TO
CONFIDENCE
OR VICE VERSA
THAT'S THE COOL PART WITH
HAPPINESS

IT'S NOT ABOUT WORDS OR
ORDER
TRUE HAPPINESS IS
A FEELING
DEMANDING TO BE
SHARED

# CHAPTER 13
## "PUBLIC OVERTURE"
by Dr. JEAN DE SERRES

Until our **PUBLIC OVERTURE**, the **HAPPY MOVIES** links and **eHappyMeditation** magazines started to work, I had to get the Strategy of 19 to work. Even if we aimed to get a star writer, a guru, I would not be betting the whole endeavor solely on Bak's reputation and success.

I tried to concentrate on ways to recruit other writers. With the idea of the 19 so-called, magazines, we thought we had a good way to start executing and recruiting new talents.

I meant, by finding 19 persons, all volunteers, paid with options so they could dream about "IF", each in charge of finding authors for their section, we would surely get to something, no?

I knew by now that Bak would deliver, or die trying. But about the others, I had to divide them into probabilities and different scenarios: let's say 5 would commit, but would never find the time or realize that they weren't made for the task. So minus 5.

13 were left, 13 who would really spend time and get involved. Of those 13, 5 would knock at every door, get a few friends admitting they always dreamed about writing (this is your chance!), and infuse them with excitement and enthusiasm to get the word out.

For a little while, we had seen texts arriving on **eHappyPedia**, but then we were in the desert. That was expected. We would have a few articles here and there and no more traffic generated, but a lot of good intentions.

5 more who would write themselves, you know, those people who buy all the chocolate bars when their kid need to sell 20 for their school. Well, they would try a few people and end up writing.

They would scratch half of their production, submit some poor articles, a few good ones, a few that would generate traffic, for a moment, and then nothing else because they lack breath and endurance. This is a tremendous individual effort to write, not momentum. Even if Bak will say otherwise…

Then you would have 4. But say we had not found 19. 19 was a target. If you are in China and you want 19, that's easy. But if you dig into your network and hope for 19, well, you must have a big pool of friends, real friends! I assumed we run short and would stop at 16.

"THE KEY IS THAT LAST PERSON"
**Dr. JEAN DE SERRES**

That leaves us with 1! I assumed that we would get 1 in 10, but we would not abandon after 10 missed fires. We would try again and again.

We needed only 1 of those people who does not write. But someone who **drives** others, NOT TO WRITE, not to do the job, but someone who **drives** (I repeat) others to create a **momentum**, to recruit more, to write a bit, to be stimulated by the first traffic, enough to get more writers.

In the American Revolution, they call it the **Paul Revere effect**! A networker and influencer. Someone who discover their own potential. Hey Bak, we need a good option package for that person!

Simple, but how do you find that person? What if that person is not in our contact list, not on our LinkedIn, not on our Facebook? I had no clue, and we just needed some luck!

To start somewhere, we used all our contact lists, and the only requirement was to share some common interest. We asked everybody to go through all their contact lists. Nothing. Now, I even wonder why we started there!

We posted on all our social media, including **eHappyPedia**! First replies were about how much it pays or is it a full-time job. And they were from abroad.

We certainly could use people from anywhere in the world, and in whatever language as long as Google translate worked for that tongue. Then, we had too many replies. The secret is that we wanted to stay vague not to give away our idea. We finally signed more than one person: they were from the 2nd category: a few articles and then nothing, not much traffic.

Some were problematic people, and one of them had to be fired. She wanted shares of the company, but she had written nothing yet! And our shares were worth nothing yet. She asked for fringe benefits, but obviously, she didn't believe. We were not making money yet, and could not afford even to pay ourselves.

Some postings were problematic. This is picky. How do you remove content? On which basis? My morale, yours? In this case, it is the complaints that drove our attention to the post.

We were NOT reading every post. Good point in a sense, but that caused a problem. Guns are not happiness! And the complaint (actually, there was only one, and it was a post) required attention.

First, we needed to drive complaints OUT of the posting section, and it was obvious that there was no other place. We had to create a complaint channel, which we did. And we thought about creating an ethic committee, but how can you find the people who have the absolute ethic?

Do they even exist? Or was the size of the business threatened to be the driver of decision? Sounds bad but not worst than having someone pretending to be better in ethics.

I consulted University professors and members of ethics committees: their conclusion was that we still had no better option than an ethic committee. But we had no money, so I suggested we hire students in ethics from different backgrounds, countries, religions. We thus created a group of people who would volunteer to argue why something should be withdrawn or NOT. We were NOT asking them to decide. Committee advise, Management decides !

But the committee still needed directions. My easy way out was to give them principles: transparency, honesty, focus on happiness. And I asked them to propose directions! They would work on it for months!

We also needed more posts, always more posts. And for that, we needed to stimulate our writers, the 19 of them (or 14 at the time)! Although that seemed the toughest part, it became easy.

The key was to focus on happiness while staying out of clichés. My job was to ask, more details, more ideas, more outputs. It seemed to be working out.

During this time, we were also working with Bak to develop more presentations, interviews, more exposure. We had to solve the issues with the links to the happiness movies and to the **eHappyMeditation**.

Those were mostly debugging challenges, but someone was needed to decide between options from 3 different programmers, and to decide between the expensive way and the cheapest but more riskier ones.

And then we had a spike in hits! This time, nothing we paid for! Just a few days with a sharp increase in volume. And the trend was constant, a nice uphill road. **eHappyPedia** seemed to attract an audience. Telling the story is making it happen.

This is **eHappyPedia, THE RISE OF THE UNICORN.**

HAPPINESS IS A
STATE OF MIND
THAT EMPOWERS
OUR BELIEFS

HAPPINESS IS THE FIRST STEP TO
CONFIDENCE
OR VICE-VERSA
THAT'S THE COOL PART WITH
HAPPINESS

IT'S NOT ABOUT WORDS OR
ORDER
TRUE HAPPINESS IS
A FEELING
DEMANDING TO BE
SHARED

# CHAPTER 14
## "A NUMBER'S GAME"

by Dr. BAK NGUYEN

I woke up one morning finding a suggested post on Facebook: the English version to the first promotional video of eHappyPedia. I watched it completely: it was a nice one, even 3 years later.

I shared it as a token of the past and a reminder for the future. Then, another memory was suggested: a video celebrating eHappyPedia reaching 1 million views over 4 weeks.

The million views were the combined views of all the versions of the promotional videos (8 languages). They were basically the same video but in each of the 8 most used languages on the web: English - French - Spanish - Mandarin (Chinese) - Portuguese - Russian - Hindi - Japanese.

The coolest part was that people were not just watching, they were responding, with 32k likes on our posts! Real numbers not neglectable. Numbers we could build from.

"FIRST RULE OF THE NEW ECONOMY:
AWARENESS FIRST AND THEN TRAFFIC."
Dr. BAK NGUYEN

You all read Jean's thoughts about how to make this work. With 2 Millions we could gamble on an idea until we might run out of cash. With 20 Millions, we were building a lasting enterprise. This was our target.

But Jean had sadly scheduled a meeting that was going to dampen our joy: the finance committee! And the numbers weren't that great. Simply put, our expenses were growing faster than our revenues.

Even with our volunteering (yes, we were not giving ourselves any salary yet), even if we were rent free, borrowing living rooms and offices from my other company. We cut the cost wherever it was possible, but still, the expenses were piling up!

We had realized that we needed to buy more capacity, more bandwidth, more computers, more programmers. To support growth, one needs to grow!

Our biggest fear was a run-down, a failure because of success! A liquidity crash ! It would be so ironic to die from the weight of our success! So we had to plan for the best and the worst scenario.

We were still not selling data. Personal data, that is! Jean did not want us to do that, but this was the key to success and the business model of every social media platform.

His thoughts were that not doing it would pay back someday, when a big scandal would turn people away from the sites abusing this revenue stream. And he was philosophically against it. He challenged me to find a different revenue stream, a creative one. I was still scratching my head about that one.

The traffic was attracting the attention of potential investors, bankers. The question was how much of the equity of the company would be given away with that injection of cash.

There was a government program helping would-be Unicorns. This meant moving into a hub designed for startup HiTech companies like gaming, Apps or Social Media.

To be eligible, we needed to be within 24 months of generating revenues and not profitable yet. We needed the capacity to grow quickly and create jobs. Those programs are meant above all, and foremost to create jobs! That was us!

At about the same time, I managed to have a bank to commit up to a quarter-million in sponsorship with some strings attached, matching every dollar we would receive from the federal government.

With an excellent interest rate, that quarter-million wasn't a debt, it was sponsorship! And with twice a quarter million in sponsorship, I could aim for an even bigger market.

The government sponsorship was actually valid only to reach a specific demography. Ours was 1.8 Million university students in Canada.

It might be 1.8 Million only, but that demography, I know how they react and how they share and what will move them. Let's do the maths and assume that most of them have 500 friends on Facebook. With the new Facebook's logarithm, only a portion of those 500 friends would see their post, probably 1%. So 1 Million user shares within their Facebook profile x 5 friends equals what?

But in my experience, it takes patience to get government money! And we still needed more money to develop, maintain and secure the platform. And we were still bleeding money !

So I went out and ask for more companies looking for the same demography for more sponsorship. A quarter-million was now the entrance ticket, half a million and a million were now how we were addressing our prospect partners.

We still needed our 20 Million investment and the paper money was not in for real but the financial statement were starting to look black! For the first time!

One victory at a time! I smiled and offered Jean a glass of champaign! We went on the piano and celebrated that long waited success!

This is **eHappyPedia, THE RISE OF THE UNICORN.** Are you ready for a better tomorrow? I Am!

HAPPINESS IS A
STATE OF MIND
THAT EMPOWERS
OUR BELIEFS

HAPPINESS IS THE FIRST STEP TO
CONFIDENCE
OR VICE VERSA
THAT'S THE COOL PART WITH
HAPPINESS

IT'S NOT ABOUT WORDS OR
ORDER
TRUE HAPPINESS IS
A FEELING
DEMANDING TO BE
SHARED

# CHAPTER 15
## "BEEFING UP"

by Dr. JEAN DE SERRES

The sponsorships gave us a pause in our bleeding. But we had no real lead for our 20M$ investment, but now, we knew how that money would help. Funny though don't you think?

We had guests (users) and clients (sponsors). The key was to keep both of them coming back at the site and the table. But I had more on my plate, to secure the investors, our only way to stay afloat and stable enough to grow a sustainable enterprise.

At the beginning, the use of that money was not so obvious! I mean, it was not clear how we would spend it and generate significant revenues.

There was the idea that we could buy traffic but that, in itself, was never enough for me. It was more like a pyramidal scheme: you pay to generate the traffic, and you can raise money because of that traffic, which can help you grow the traffic, etc.

But, now that our **HAPPY MOVIES** link, our eHappyMeditation magazine (yes, it was the first of the 19 magazines to really get some serious traffic), our first few postings of this book generated traffic. I knew we could generate traffic, not just buy it. Not to forget the home run in the universities, we were certain that we had a chance to last!

I went on to spend time on a detailed financial plan. The first step was done with a friend specialized in web advertising, and we estimated the number of views we could generate, the time per view, the clicks.

We assumed a certain level of success (2 magazines out of 19), a certain level of synergy with the references between sites and links, a certain level of advertising.

We dug the internet to find numbers. We looked at all public information in companies Annual Reports and presentations. We did not buy those data simply because there were too expensive. So we guessed here and there.

The important point was that we documented all our guesses in a spreadsheet, and we documented all our references so that the serious investor could challenge our model or beef it up with his own info.

We had to work on the value of the data collected. Sincerely, it was the value of the data that drove the brainstorm on which data to collect. But after reading a book on creating totally new markets, like Pfizer did with Viagra, or like Facebook did, we decided some not valuable info would actually find value later on! That was a new assumption in our long list of assumptions.

Although we were lean, we were still expensive in our growth. I finally had a better idea of the cost of programming, networking, hosting, etc. We had detailed plans on the productivity of our employees, and we could guess our manpower cost for the future.

Then I got to the excel spreadsheet. This was the key moment. This one would take days to finalize. I kept asking Bak: how much will it cost you to buy X number of computers, to buy X capacity on the web, to buy X links with Facebook?

There were so many variables. I need a number, I need a formula, one I could adjust later on to fit the needs and the requirement of each investor. And yes, some investors can be very specific about their ways of doing things and of calculating.

To answer these questions, we needed to forecast our traffic, our use of data. Bak's estimates are always very optimistic. I got used to slash his prediction by factors (yes, factors) to make a case for the competition, for the unavoidable delays, for the hidden cost.

How much tax would we pay? Did we budget the spending on training since it is mandatory to spend at least 1%? Did we budget the accountants, the lawyers? How about international revenues?

Where do we pay our taxes, and how do we avoid paying double taxes? How can we reduce the legal fees? These were discussions at $1000/hour rate! But they all needed to be addressed.

We needed to pay to protect the trademark, the insurance, the sickness leaves, the recruitment. Oh, and by the way, whenever you have more than three staff, you need management, top management.

Top management is heavy on the burn rate unless you give lots of options which cost nothing for the immediate time, but cost much on the value of the future. So I made new assumptions about staffing. How many more programmers will we need with the increased traffic, with new attacks from hackers, with new bugs unavoidable with each update?

How much expense will we need to pay for those **FAMOUS 19**? When do we pay them? At the recruitment? The delivering? Do we pay on production or on the performance of the article produced?

Will they charge us for their internet bill or the price of a laptop? How much reserve do we put for our first conflict with one of the **FAMOUS 19**?

Litigation! That's a classic. When someone claims to own more shares of the company, someone on disability while working on a volunteer basis, but not quite volunteer because of the given options. Isn't it equivalent to a pay check, to an employee status? You'll be surprised how much resources and energy those matters can swallow!

Moreover, we had to make really good assumptions about the value of the traffic. How much is a hit worth? How likely is it that this hit will be recurrent to drive friends or to influence people at the other end of the world? All the reasons are good to generate interest and traffic to our platform, **eHappyPedia**.

I knew these assumptions had to be substantial because the VC would be very knowledgeable about them. They don't care if our spending budget is $1M a year or $1.1M even though 100 000$ seems a lot to you and me. What they care about is the value : $10M or $20M?

With traffic in the millions of hits, and with a capital market value being a multiple of the traffic revenue, you could guess that this is highly leveraged, can it be amplified?

$0.00001 means Millions more than $0.000001! Because there are multipliers involved ! So we read everything that was published on the subject of valuation of social media traffic. First, with the public companies: theirs 10K forms or Annual reports are saying so much.

Then, we read every presentations we could find about startups. Why is a huge pension fund investing suddenly $100M in a startup selling information about flights or hotels? Why do they say Uber is already worth $120 Billion?

"IT'S NOT THE MAIN PRODUCT LIKE A TAXI RIDE THAT DRIVES THE VALUATION BUT THE DERIVATIVES. THAT'S THE VALUE OF THE INFORMATION."

Dr. JEAN DE SERRES

This is all part of what you need to understand as a startup. How could we value the information posted, exchanged or gathered within **eHappyPedia**?

We had obviously checked with friends working in the advertisement world about current rates, but that wasn't satisfactory. Bak was talking about huge traffic, but when I compared our forecasts to, not only the winners but all startups, we were essentially saying: we will win, believe us. Our numbers needed to **beef up**.

We developed a value for the happiness market! Out of public health data, out of studies showing the importance of happiness or empowerment, out of human resources' studies showing the impact of a positive atmosphere.

I created a few assumptions by linking some concepts in management to public health concepts, to healthy living beliefs and trends. I circled the trends: yoga, meditation, spa. These trends were saying much!

First assumption : Facebook was a global phenomenon, and yet, not a key to health or happiness (see here, I was adding health to happiness, like sometimes I was adding public interest to happiness, to grow our base).

I imagined (because I could not afford surveys that would have confirmed my hypothesis) that surveys would show no association between Facebook or Instagram and HAPPINESS!

In a presentation, when you don't have data supporting your claims, you trick it: you ask the question. Do you think Facebook is the face of happiness? Of course not!

Or you can just state your UNSUPPORTED claim, and it works most of the time because you had data in the prior claim: X Millions of people are depressed, X Millions are doing yoga to find peace.

"AFTER PEACE, HAPPINESS IS NEXT."
Dr. JEAN DE SERRES

That happiness message is a winner! Our world is growing economically, but it is also less and less happy. If you have doubts, look at the manifestation of the unhappy people in France, the *GILETS JAUNES'* movement, they are the polarization in our democracies. And this is just one example.

A lack of happiness, no face or name to canalize happiness, no symbol of any movement of Happiness of any sort. Ironic, no? While for most of our life, we sacrifice, work and struggle with the promise of finding happiness one day!

Actually, that movement did not exist, but we needed it to exist! The VC would believe that it needed to exist too. They would see how vast the market is.

**eHappyPedia** needs to prove that it can be the emblem of the happiness, a movement joining the green movement, the disillusioned people, the crowd that succeeded financially, the governments in need of stability.

Dr. JEAN DE SERRES

We needed the traffic though, to establish the image, but we should value the company to the success of the movement, and to **eHappyPedia** being the key to that movement.

Actually, I know that we started with the idea of an encyclopedia of Happiness. But by now, it was obvious, we needed a movement of happiness, not just an encyclopedia. So we would refer to it as **eHappy**!

Right now, I am having 5 million views and 32k likes from Facebook and You Tube. **BUT OUR VALUE IS MORE THAN CLICK'S POTENTIAL, it is THE MARKET TO BE CREATED** !

I entered some numbers in the excel spreadsheet, adjusted the formulas: it's always a more extensive work than what it seems at the beginning because you always find new ways and numbers…

In short, it is a work in progress, and by finding mistakes, I knew that we were evolving towards something solid. I made forecasts for spending and revenues, and VALUE for 10 years, added several scenarios that were changing the numbers dramatically.

I isolated all the key numbers under hypothesis so a VC could say, I don't like your inflation at 2%, let's make it 1% or 3% and see the impact.

Then we defined the request: 20M$ investment as initial investment followed by more investments over the next 5 to 7 years. Keep in mind how long it took Amazon to become profitable! All those years, someone has to invest money to pay the bills!!!

Each new investor is diluting the first ones, and we assume they were joining at a lower risk, so they are paying a higher price for their equity. It took days to finalize the spreadsheet, but now we had calculations to support our numbers!

For a VC speed-meeting hundreds of startups like us, all saying they have the perfect recipe for success, how do we make sure that they will remember us? How do we differentiate ourselves?

I was saying that our concept was nice, playing on similar scale, but like a song among thousands of songs, still unique.
Now we believe we not only have a winner, we have a definition of it, the concept AND the MARKET !

Bak is the face of the company, a winner within some crowds. Can he convince the crowd of VCs? We have great numbers with the assumption that happiness is a new market with a strong brand name. Bak, did we protect the trademark all around the world? Oops, we have it only in a few places. The cost to cover the planet was…

I was now confident enough to ask 50% for 20M$ investment, knowing we would be happy with 20% or even 10%.We had checked out all companies known publicly to have invested in social media OR data.

We polished our curriculum to make them more relevant, worked on the wording of the mission to make appealing, and claimed big shares of an emerging market. That was the easy part.

I had updated our Business Plan. Much shorter this time, but with lots of meat behind it. One page to tell our story. One page to present the co-founders and introduce the **PUBLIC OVERTURE** and our book.

One page with financials summarized. One page with the ask. A backup page with the use of money. That's it! They would either like the story or not. The numbers were there only to show that we knew what we were doing. And they would buy only if they bought the image and chief-marketer Bak and the manager Jean.

So we sent it to all who could be possibly interested. And now, I needed Bak to make a marketing coup. Why not Oprah I said? Or something!

Something that would come to the ears of a VC who will want to talk to us and then we pull out our Business Plan he probably received but didn't read. And then we're on…

Meanwhile, I had planned a tour of the VCs (Venture Capitalists) in New York City, the home of Wall Street, Silicon Valley, in California as well as Seattle. And for the form, a few in Montreal.

This is **eHappyPedia, THE RISE OF THE UNICORN.**

HAPPINESS IS A
STATE OF MIND
THAT EMPOWERS
OUR BELIEFS

HAPPINESS IS THE FIRST STEP TO
CONFIDENCE
OR VICE VERSA
THAT'S THE COOL PART WITH
HAPPINESS

IT'S NOT ABOUT WORDS OR
ORDER
TRUE HAPPINESS IS
A FEELING
DEMANDING TO BE
SHARED

# CHAPTER 16
## "ONE BILLION"

by Dr. BAK NGUYEN

While Jean was leading the investment project, I was occupied with marketing and Public Relations. My job is to create value and more value. The only way I know to create value is from attention and relationship. Show people something there can relate to, show them the potential and empower them to make the difference.

A few days have passed since I met with my new friend, Anil Gupta. We had met during my event in front of a half-full room, in an event that started slow but ended as a success.

Between the crazy schedule and the advancement of my ongoing projects, I pushed for the completion of the **UAX, ULTIMATE AUDIO EXPERIENCE** of **CHANGING THE WOLRD FROM A DENTAL CHAIR**.

I was now aiming to deliver not only a great experience to the users but to empower authors and influencers like Dr. Anil Gupta, Sir Richard Branson, Champion Mike Tyson, motivational speaker Anthony Robbins, theirs friends and audiences. The odds on the table were tremendous!

I got my creative director in, Justin Morganstein, to fast track the end of the production for my last event that had bee filmed to that end. A week later, we were done!

I listened and re-listened to the whole experience and, in my opinion, it was flawless! The best experience I had was while driving. From a Bose surround system, the **UAX**'s experience sounded terrific!

Now, all I needed to do was to make it available online and have Dr. Anil Gupta try the experience from the comfort of his home, in the

USA. Everything was moving so fast. Yes, it is pretty rare that I say that things are moving too fast, but really, they are! Finally!

I tasked Justin to publish the **UAX** of **CHANGING THE WORLD FROM A DENTAL CHAIR** on both Spotify and iTunes. Yes, we are more than an audiobook, we are an experience, entertaining, appealing and with educational value!

To submit our tracks proved to be harder than we expected. We were more than an audiobook and we were not music. To categorize the **UAX**'s track wasn't a simple task. It took us a few months to finally got accepted. It was a long and slow process. Everything normal feels like an eternity…

In the midst of the excitement, Jean and I finally found a time to sit down and to consult about the writing of our book, our company, our endeavor. I told him about Dr. Anil, and he was impressed.

Actually, Jean is never impressed, he is polite, then, he starts to ask questions and to poke around to understand the truth. Always respectfully, but he will test before he believes.

Me, I am a believer! I got him through what happened within the last weeks, walked him through the advancement of **UAX** and the interest I got from Dr. Anil Gupta.

I forgot to tell you that Jean didn't know about the **UAX** project, which is independent of the **eHappy** journey. That was one of my pet project on the side. But now, we had created a synergy between both projects to finally get the win we were hoping for.

Until lately, I was concentring all of my efforts towards generating traffic and getting people's interest. Let's talk numbers. Knowing that Dr. Gupta is looking to reach 1 billion people by the end of next year and that he has already reached 45 million people until now, I had a great proposal to make to help him.

He has a great message, author of the immediate recipe for happiness. With the **UAX**, I have a sexy and very cool medium to spread the word. If we combined them together, we have a home run, a great message and a cool medium.

Out of respect for our partners and NDA signed, I can only share this much: I would provide him through **UAX** an additional reach of about 6 million people, from the **eHappy** market, mostly university students. OK, that's only 7% of a billion, way behind his goal, but still...

So yes, it is realistic and can be done. The last time we spoke, I promised him my help, let's push further. The web is all about connectivity.

Knowing Dr. Anil Gupta would give certain advices for people to turn their lives around within weeks, and knowing that this would require a place for people to *"deposit"* their goodwill and their engagement towards themselves, I saw the opportunity for eHappy.

On that, trust me. This is really how anyone can start changing their lives, by writing down their thoughts and by sharing them. I wrote a whole book on the matter, my 8th book, **MOMENTUM TRANSFER**.

So if Anil can have his audience to commit and to publish their own will to change, **eHappyPedia** can be the perfect tool to help him keep contact with his audience.

Because it is the best way to multiply your reach, **eHappyPedia** is a great tool to publish from. Whatever you write there is edited and polished as an article coming out of a magazine. So people look good, writing. If they look good writing, they will share.

"WRITING WITHOUT SHARING HOLDS VERY LITTLE POWER."
Dr. BAK NGUYEN

His reach of 45 millions is only the first generation. Plus the 6 millions I was promising him and with each referring up to 10 people, I estimated 51 million people for the 2nd generation. Even if we think that only 1% of his audience would answer the call to write on **eHappyPedia**, that is still 510K people.

"THE POWER OF EHAPPY IS THAT IT IS BOTH
A POWERFUL EDITING TOOL AND A GREAT PUBLISHING ENHANCER."
Dr. BAK NGUYEN

Oh, yes, that's only a fraction of Dr. Anil's mission to reach 1 billion lives.

Knowing Dr. Anil, he won't be stopping there. In parallel with this **eHappy/UAX** effort, he will still be pushing with his conventional means too. Let push it a step further, shall we?

What would be the next logical step to take? If I was Dr. Gupta, I would be asking my friends to contribute and to answer my call of action. If Sir Richard Branson, Anthony Robbins and Mike Tyson are answering the call, by themselves, using the same funnel, imagine the numbers!

What we might have to do is a new video embedded within each article showing Dr. Anil with Sir Branson, Mike Tyson and Anthony Robbins, if they accept our proposal. **TO HELP THE WORLD BE HAPPY**, who would say no to that?

Oh yes, I will negotiate a spot for Jean and myself to say hi to the world and invite them to embrace the great vibe: **IMMEDIATE HAPPINESS!**

"WHEN ONE FEELS UNHAPPY, DON'T COMPLAIN, KEEP PUSHING UNTIL THE WEATHER, THE ENVIRONMENT, EVEN TIME HAS CHANGED, AND THEN, FEEL PLEASED."

Dr. BAK NGUYEN

**eHappyPedia** is a very powerful tool. This time, I had the chance to put it to a real test since I am seconding a man with a huge and noble mission, to improve 1 billion lives within the next year and a half. He has the will, we have the tools and the means.

Jean wanted a movement of **HAPPINESS**. Anil wrote an **IMMEDIATE RECIPE FOR HAPPINESS**. Why not make everyone happy? Really, why

213

not make everyone happy, Dr. De Serres, Dr. Gupta, the investors and 1 Billion people by the same occasion?

"I WON'T STOP UNTIL YOU, UNTIL WE, UNTIL I AM HAPPY."
**Dr. BAK NGUYEN**

This is the promise. One Billion is the new goal and happiness is the prize! This is **eHappy, THE RISE OF THE UNICORN**. Are you ready for a better tomorrow? I Am!

HAPPINESS IS A
STATE OF MIND
THAT EMPOWERS
OUR BELIEFS

HAPPINESS IS THE FIRST STEP TO
CONFIDENCE
OR VICE VERSA
THAT'S THE COOL PART WITH
HAPPINESS

IT'S NOT ABOUT WORDS OR
ORDER
TRUE HAPPINESS IS
A FEELING
DEMANDING TO BE
SHARED

# CHAPTER 17
## "THE RISE OF THE UNICORN"
by Dr. JEAN DE SERRES

That day in New York City was both fun and hectic. Fun because going from one office to the next in NYC makes you feel like you are in a movie. Hectic because we had five meetings scheduled and some taxi-hailing in between to rush from one place to the next.

Those VCs are surprising: lots of money, small offices and most of them did not let you use your slides. But we had paper versions of the presentation and the business plan! I knew how to prepare for it, so we had our story ready!

I insisted we rehearse the presentation like a play. It took two days and a few friends as critics. With a whiteboard and many paper sheets aligned on the walls, divided in each section of the presentation and business plan. Each line had to be natural but prepared. Each word had to prepare the launch of a message.

We had essentially 15 minutes of play and 30 minutes of improvisation. Even for improvisation, the questions or discussion period was just an opportunity to present one of the numerous answers that we prepared for.

We knew the source of each data, and when no data was supporting a point, we had a sentence with an image to explain it. Followed by a second sentence driving the audience to the next point we wanted to focus on.

This is speed dating: seduction happens or not, little foreplay where we tried to bounce back their questions about travelling or the weather, only to invite them to open up and to talk about themselves.

Here, I voluntarily used each important word 3 times. When one of us is talking, the other's mission is to spot the weakness, the anger and the positive signs. We would never interrupt each other, trusting each other to follow the scenario or had a good reason to steer away from it.

The first group looked simply uninterested! I decided to claim it as a practice. One group was clear about a follow-up. We didn't know about our impact on the others.

One group was so grounded in that field that their questions were right on our weak spots. I thought that the group would end up being the one. We shook hands with high hopes.

But for now, it was time to fly to California, and then Seattle. Hey, we had practice, and the trip is fun in good company! That's one of the advantages of getting along well with your partners!

We arrived a day in advance, brushing up in the morning, wondering if we should look relax taking in some of the California sun! Bak was always up an hour earlier to find a spot to write near the pool. If you wanted to look for him, look for the sunniest spot!

California style or tie and London gentleman? We choose the relaxed style with a tie ready, just in case. Does the dressing matters, the look? I believe it will make a first impression, but it's probably the look with the style of the person that matters, and we can't change our style so easily. Better look genuine!

Should we have adjusted our presentation from one city to another? Maybe, but we choose not to. Our scenario was so tight and well balanced. And then we had to wait.

3 VCs got back to us with questions, not the ones that I thought were interested in. And the 3 of them asks us to redo our calculations in a different format. Which we did.

Following on a few questions, a few calls on our business plan, all on the action part, I sensed that one of them wanted to add some staff of their own. We were open.

At this stage, it's better to be open, to not frighten them. Yes, it may seem from the Facebook's history that you can be harsh and strong on your position, but I guess the facts would show this usually leads to the end of the discussion, where most projects never get the much-needed investment, so don't piss off the investors.

It took three months of calls, emails to get a first offer, and it was not that good: $5 million for 90% of the business! I was happy, Bak was not. I pushed for more discussions.

Our strategy was to negotiate a deal with them slowly with the hope that someone else would beat them. And we aimed at $5M for 60%. We were about to lose control of our baby.

The Facebook story was saying, don't do it! Ask for more, aim for more. But $5M was getting us full time with the company, and we had a real chance to do something. And of course, more money would follow if we had early success.

But then we would get even more diluted said Bak, to 20 or even 10%! There is no perfect answer. It's a gamble. Yes, a gamble. Some studies have shown that the perception of people is biased by the movies: people generally believe that they have greater chances to survive a shooting wound because they saw it so many times with their favorite heroes.

As a doctor, I can tell you how biased they are, unfortunately. They believe their chances of winning are higher because of the publicity and the movies. That single story is pointing out the cinderella story.

You heard about Facebook Zuckerberg refusing 200 million dollars for his company early on, and winning that bet, so you think you can do the same.

But you don't know if he was 1 winner out of 2 bets or million, which is likely the case! And who is reading about the other 999 999 stories of great ideas?

We started the review of the contract they proposed while we made a counteroffer at $5 million for 75%. It was close to a deception, which is a danger for the investors as well, they need a motivated leadership team. As for us, we would still have 25% to grow.

We reviewed the contract for weeks, tweaking it here and there, waiting for the next teleconference where they would ask a little change in the plan and the valuation.

During the months of discussion, following the leads of the **HAPPY MOVIES**, **eHappyMeditation** and the **PUBLIC OVERTURE**, our traffic had kept growing and those months of growth created value.

But another key event was when Bak's friend posted an article about the **PUBLIC OVERTURE**! And he quoted the **RISE OF THE UNICORN**, the book in process.

Suddenly, the readings on the postings of the first paragraph jumped sky-high. We even started to have a dialogue with a few people offering advice.

Advice is good, but the best thing was the offer to fly to Phoenix to meet an investor interested in our project. We even wrote about it on a post, and then, investors started talking about it. And we got a few more requests for meetings, one of them we met in NYC earlier.

We didn't realize the size of the traffic until the servers crashed, but then our chief engineer was so quick to find a solution with one Cloud provider that Bak and I didn't have time to react. We have a great team of dedicated people.

Let's step back for a second: over the previous months, we had built a much better content. Our Strategy of 19 worked, and we actually had two so-called success, none however big enough to declare Victory, but enough to have solid content posting day after day.

These two staffs were leveraging their network like crazy, multiplying the calls to dozens of people who each had TOTALLY different networks, but all were hitting on the need to describe happiness and ways to happiness. Moreover, we now had many volunteers proposing their services, and we could see a number of new magazines to be created.

We had a number of women's magazines talking about our site in their columns, and that was the main payment for most of our writers: an audience.

And then, **eHappyMeditation** was catching up as the place to go to for a site with no advertisement! The **HAPPY MOVIES** still grew steadily and to tell the truth, we had become addicted to those movies ourselves.

A first journalist did an article about us. The article was replicated on Apple News. And we were suddenly regularly in the news. Not just the news, but Happiness discussions.People started debating about it, moralizing about it, analyzing it with psychology, spirituality, with economics, even anthropology. Where does happiness bring us? Is it the destination or the journey? Is it going to make us lazy? Is it compatible with religion? Is it too much, is there too much?

My son had just completed his thesis on a related-theme, and we posted it on **eHappyPedia**. It was followed by hundreds of articles and thesis on multiple hypothesis. It could be about communism and the quest for happiness, or sex and drugs vs happiness.

But mostly, within days we had commercial links, by the thousands. We were suddenly short of staff, even with all the friends and family we called to the rescue.

We had to find creative ways to link back to the advertisers without upsetting the users. We decided it had to be through related posts, not written by the industry, but by some current users of the product.

Do you want an ad? Find me a happy customer of yours, declare that you never paid that person in whatsoever creative way, and we will interview that person to make a post about the product and happiness.

That was a part of our new business model! No direct publicity. No ads. But articles by your users and instructions on where to shop for it. You pay a lump sum initially, no direct relation with the traffic of your *not-yours* article.

You decide what to pay us every month, and we decide if it is enough. No one is paid to fool the customer. We inform only, and we give a chance to happiness.

That suited us like a suit, since Bak and I are both doctors, one in dentistry and one in medicine all swore to protect our patients first. This was a smile from the universe!

Our bank had to quickly expand our credit margins, but the noise was so big by now that we didn't have to negotiate anymore. The numbers were changing by the hours since the offers start raining in.

And we went back to the table to discuss the offers. We asked for 20M$ for 50% of the company. We were a unicorn, a billion-dollar company to be.

This is no movie, this is **eHappyPedia, THE RISE OF THE UNICORN**.

HAPPINESS IS A
STATE OF MIND
THAT EMPOWERS
OUR BELIEFS

HAPPINESS IS THE FIRST STEP TO
CONFIDENCE
OR VICE VERSA
THAT'S THE COOL PART WITH
HAPPINESS

ITS NOT ABOUT WORD WOR
ORDER
TRUE HAPPINESS IS
A FEELING
DEMANDING TO BE
SHARED

# CONCLUSION

by Dr. JEAN DE SERRES

Creating, telling a story, building a company are similar in many ways. I don't know if friendship is. Maybe it is after all: you have hope, you get frustrated sometimes, you stray, you get back on focus, you invest, you take the return.

When you're dead, the important things are those you have left for the prosperity. When you're alive, it is the relationship with others around you and what you are creating (not what's left). In this sense, the process is really of importance.

TELLING THE STORY IS THE OUTPUT

Dr. JEAN DE SERRES

At the beginning of **eHappyPedia**, we looked for ways to do something meaningful for us individually, and together as much as for the world. It was clear to us that the celebration of happiness was not well covered.

That happiness is not just about victory. After all, there is only one winner out of dozens if not thousands of participants! That happiness is not just about overachieving. After all, you cannot beat yourself every day!

That happiness is not just about a specific day in the year. Why only for my birthday? But that happiness is about every day, every moment, every individual, as a celebration of life and of being human.

A celebration that we are not the most violent and aggressive species on the planet that we are mostly social and the happy at our core. Because happiness is a quality and a winning one.

Writing this book was a particular experience on its own. Special because none of us, Bak neither I, were sure what to expect or where it would lead.

We are both doctors and both teacher, in our own ways. To help is our natural, to train and inspire others, a second nature. Well, now that I am writing the final words of the great journey, I have to tell you that it was exactly that: we shared to help, and from the process, we empowered and inspired you.

Bak started this book revealing that it was my attempt to bring back one of his dormant projects back at the center of both our attentions. We are men of our words, and we do as we say.

Writing this book allowed both of us to relive the why of the how **eHappyPedia** came to life. Writing this book allowed us to mash up reality and projections, to both simulate and test a possible outcome, a near future.

80% of the facts related in the previous chapters are what we did and the people we met. The other 20%, well, those are the simulated and projected thoughts. This is not deceiving, it is projecting.

The goal of this journey was to share with you how to rise a Unicorn. To us, it was the reminder that **eHappyPedia** is worth ur time and passion.

At the time of this writing, not all that we related in within these pages had happened yet. But now that we have such a clear vision, it will.

If you pick you the book as our first readers, we thank you for your interest and faith in us. This is also why we both want to clarify our position about reality.

We don't know when you will be reading this story. Google search **eHappyPedia**, Dr. Bak or Dr. Jean De Serres to know where we are in our quest. This is no fiction, it is our reality, we simply mixed up the tense of the verbs, making the past, the future and the present into a whole, a great story.

Bak said that knowledge is of the past, and happiness about the future. I like to live. Mediation has no past, future, nor present. So to build and to bridge from our differences, we baked a cake blending future, past and present into one.

This is our story. Have your own version of it, have a piece of it, and above all, may you find your happiness with whatever you found!

This is **eHappyPedia, THE RISE OF THE UNICORN.** Are you ready for a better tomorrow? To be continued…

HAPPINESS IS A
STATE OF MIND
THAT EMPOWERS
OUR BELIEFS

HAPPINESS IS THE FIRST STEP TO
CONFIDENCE
OR VICE VERSA
THAT'S THE COOL PART WITH
HAPPINESS

IT'S NOT ABOUT WORDS OR
ORDER
TRUE HAPPINESS IS
A FEELING
DEMANDING TO BE
SHARED

# ABOUT THE AUTHORS

From Canada, **Dr BAK NGUYEN**, Nominee Ernst and Young Entrepreneur of the year, Grand Homage Lys DIVERSITY, and LinkedIn & TownHall Achiever of the year. Dr Bak is a cosmetic dentist, CEO and founder of Mdex & Co. His company is revolutionizing the dental field. Speaker and motivator, he wrote 72 books over 36 months accumulating many world records (to be officialized).

- **ENTREPRENEURSHIP**
- **LEADERSHIP**
- **QUEST OF IDENTITY**
- **DENTISTRY AND MEDICINE**
- **PARENTING**
- **CHILDREN BOOKS**
- **PHILOSOPHY**

In 2003, he founded Mdex, a dental company upon which in 2018, he launched the most ambitious private endeavour to reform the dental industry, Canada wide. Philosopher, he has close to his heart the quest of happiness of the people surrounding him, patients and colleagues alike. In 2020, he launched an International collaborative initiative named **THE ALPHAS** to share knowledge and for Entrepreneurs and Doctors to thrive through the Greatest Pandemic and Economic depression of our time.

In 2016, he co-found with Tranie Vo, Emotive World Incorporated, a tech research company to use technology to empower happiness and sharing. U.A.X. the ultimate audio experience is the landmark project on which the team is advancing, utilizing the technics of the movie industry and the advancement in ARTIFICIAL INTELLIGENCE to save the book industry and to upgrade the continuing education space.

These projects have allowed Dr Nguyen to attract interests from the international and diplomatic community and he is now the center of a global discussion in the wellbeing and the future of the health profession. It is in that matter that he shares his thoughts and encourages the health community to share their own stories.

*"It's not worth it go through it alone! Together, we stand, alone, we fall."*

Motivational speaker and serial entrepreneur, philosopher and author, from his own words, Dr Nguyen describes himself as a dentist by circumstances, an entrepreneur by nature and a communicator by passion.

He also holds recognitions from the Canadian Parliament and the Canadian Senate.

www.DrBakNguyen.com

From Canada, **Dr. JEAN DE SERRES**, ESG/UQAM, MANAGER OF THE YEAR. Dr. De Serres is a MD with MBA and Master degree in public health. He has been a family physician, a CEO, a board administrator, an entrepreneur, a speaker and a teacher. Dr. De Serres is the former CEO of Hema Quebec.

He also created a clinic for victims of sexual abuse. Currently VP in a pharmaceutical company, his main focus is the change of organizational culture and innovation.

# UAX

## ULTIMATE AUDIO EXPERIENCE

A new way to learn and enjoy Audiobooks. Made to be entertaining while keeping the self-educational value of a book, UAX will appeal to both auditive and visual people. UAX is the blockbuster of the Audiobooks.

UAX will cover most of Dr Bak's books, and is now negotiating to bring more authors and more titles to the UAX concept. Now streaming on Spotify, Apple Music and available for download on all major music platforms. Give it a try today!

AMAZON - BARNES & NOBLE - APPLE BOOKS - KINDLE
SPOTIFY - APPLE MUSIC

# C O M B O
## PAPERBACK/AUDIOBOOK
### ACTIVATION

Please register your book to receive the link to your audiobook version. Register at:
https://baknguyen.com/unicorn-registry

# FROM THE SAME AUTHOR
### Dr Bak Nguyen

www.DrBakNguyen.com

MAJOR LEAGUES' ACCESS

**FACTEUR HUMAIN** -032
LE LEADERSHIP DU SUCCÈS
par Dr. BAK NGUYEN & CHRISTIAN TRUDEAU

**ehappyPedia** -037
THE RISE OF THE UNICORN
BY Dr. BAK NGUYEN & Dr. JEAN DE SERRES

**CHAMPION MINDSET** -038
LEARNING TO WIN
BY Dr. BAK NGUYEN & CHRISTOPHE MULUMBA

**BRANDING DrBAK** -039
BALANCING STRATEGY AND EMOTIONS
BY Dr. BAK NGUYEN

002 - **La Symphonie des Sens**
ENTREPREUNARIAT
par Dr. BAK NGUYEN

006 - **Industries Disruptors**
BY Dr .BAK NGUYEN

007 - **Changing the World
from a dental chair**
BY Dr. BAK NGUYEN

008 - **The Power Behind the Alpha**
BY TRANIE VO & Dr. BAK NGUYEN

035 - **SELFMADE**
GRATITUDE AND HUMILITY
BY Dr. BAK NGUYEN

072 - **THE U.A.X. STORY**
THE ULTIMATE AUDIO EXPERIENCE
BY Dr. BAK NGUYEN

BUSINESS

**SYMPHONY OF SKILLS** -001
BY Dr. BAK NGUYEN

# CHILDREN'S BOOK
with William Bak

## The Trilogy of Legends

# DENTISTRY

LIFESTYLE

QUEST OF IDENTITY

MILLION DOLLAR MINDSET

DR.

*Bak Nguyen*

www.ingramcontent.com/pod-product-compliance
Lightning Source LLC
Chambersburg PA
CBHW061153220326
41599CB00025B/4468